JULIETTE LOW

Illustrated by

JANE CASTLE

JULIETTE LOW

by
MILDRED MASTIN PACE

Edited and with an Introduction by
DANNY L. MILLER

The Jesse Stuart Foundation
Ashland, Kentucky
1997

JULIETTE LOW

Library of Congress Cataloging-in-Publication Data

Pace, Mildred Mastin.
    Juliette Low / by Mildred Mastin Pace ; edited and with an introduction by Danny L. Miller.
        p.   cm.
    Originally published : New York : C. Scribner's, 1947.
    Summary : Traces the life of the founder of the Girl Scouts in America from her girlhood in Savannah, Georgia during the Civil War to her death in 1927.
    ISBN 0-945084-61-7
    1. Low, Juliette Gordon, 1860-1927--Juvenile literature. 2. Girl Scouts of the United States of America--Biography--Juvenile literature. 3. Girl Scouts--United States--Biography--Juvenile literature. [1. Low, Juliette Gordon, 1860-1927. 2. Girl Scouts of the United States of America--Biography. 3. Women--Biography.]
    I. Miller, Danny L. II, Title.
    HS3268.2.L68P33 1997
    369.463' 092--dc21
    [B]   97-2456
                                                                        CIP
                                                                        AC

The Jesse Stuart Foundation
P. O. Box 391 Ashland, KY 41114
1997

CONTENTS

Dedicated to

Kathleen Beyer Dorman
September 24, 1953
October 21, 1991

---

*Contributions to the
Kathy Beyer Dorman Fund, which provides
books for adult new readers can be made to:*

Kathy Beyer Dorman Fund
*C/o Jesse Stuart Foundation
P.O. Box 391
Ashland, KY 41114*

INTRODUCTION

Mildred Mastin Pace was born June 8, 1907 in St. Louis, Missouri, the daughter of Robert Thomas Mastin and Miriam Norris. She was married to the editor Clark Roberts Pace in 1935, and for many years they lived across the Hudson River from West Point in Garrison-on-Hudson, New York. Mrs. Pace was a magazine writer, a free-lance radio writer for the Mutual Broadcasting Company and the National Broadcasting Company in the 1920s and 30s and a publicity writer for the J. Walter Thompson advertising agency in the 1940s. During this time, she also turned her creative talents to writing non-fiction stories for young adults. She spent most of her childhood years in Kentucky and moved back there in the later years of her life; she lived on Nicholasville Road in Lexington. One of her books is a biography of the famous Kentucky race horse Exterminator, and another, her only fiction work,

Home Is Where the Heart Is, is set in the mountains of eastern Kentucky.

Mrs. Pace spent most of her literary career writing biographies for young people about figures who achieved great things in their lives and made great contributions to society, such as Clara Barton, the founder of the American Red Cross, and Henry Bergh, the founder of the American Society for the Prevention of Cruelty to Animals (ASPCA). The Jesse Stuart Foundation reprinted *Friend of Animals: The Story of Henry Bergh* in 1995. *Juliette Low* is one of those biographies of inspiring people, Juliette "Daisy" Low, the founder of the Girl Scouts of America.

It is very fitting that the Jesse Stuart Foundation should republish this book by Mildred Mastin Pace, for the Stuart Foundation is dedicated to preserving the ideals embodied by Jesse Stuart in his own writings. Jesse Stuart was a man who believed strongly in the youth of America and their potential for accomplishing great deeds. His own life story would have been one that Mrs. Pace could have used for one of her biographies.

Often in talks and essays, Jesse Stuart spoke of the unlimited opportunities open to America's young people. He praised the American character and often remarked on the fact that as a result of his travels around the world he was convinced that America offered the greatest opportunities of any nation to anyone who was willing to work. He used his own life and accomplishments as an example of how someone born in relative poverty could nevertheless rise to national and international prominence through hard work and moral character.

Jesse Stuart was committed to the development of moral character in young people, as can readily be seen in his enormously popular children's book *A Penny's Worth of Character*, as well as in countless essays and stories. I often reflect on his words about the teaching profession, one of the most important areas in the building of moral character in young people, in the Preface to *The Thread That Runs So True*, one of the most eloquent statements on the profession of teaching ever written. In it, Stuart says:

> *No one can ever tell me that education, rightly directed*
> *without propaganda, cannot change the individual, community,*
> *state, and the world for the better. It can. There must*
> *be health, science, technology, the arts, and conservation*
> *of all worthwhile things that aid humanity upon this earth.*
> *And there must be character education. (vii)*

Stuart's own life was a testimonial to the kind of character that he believed in--morality, honesty, humility, and work, the kind of character we need so badly in our world today.

In a short essay entitled "Character and the American Youth," in his collection of essays *If I Were Seventeen Again* (USA: Archer Editions Press, 1980), Stuart addresses this issue. "Character and the American youth," he says, "is a subject nearest my heart after my many years in the schoolroom, teaching hundreds of youths in secondary schools, and after speaking to approximately 40,000 university students and members of teaching groups in America" (75). In this essay, Stuart talks about the major qualities that need to be developed in young people: morals, character, integrity, and hard work. He also talks about parental involvement in their children's educations, and he fears that parents may be unintentionally harming their children. "Here," he says, "is one of the greatest mistakes parents make today. I mean parents who have had to struggle. They don't mean to hurt their children. They think they are helping them. They never want them to work as hard as they've had to work. They want life to be easier for them." But, he continues, "Children should know that the good things in life come hard. It's a sin to raise a child up and not let him know how to do work with his hands" (76).

Jesse Stuart's concern for the youth of America, their development of moral character and integrity and their recognition of the value of work to strengthen their community and our nation, was one shared by Juliette "Daisy" Low, the heroine of this book. Juliette Low believed in the development of American character and that girls and young women should be encouraged in the building of these moral qualities. The stated purpose of the Girl Scouts of America is "to meet the special needs of girls and help girls develop as happy, resourceful individuals willing to share their abilities in their homes, their communities, their country, and the world" (*Encyclopedia of Associations*, 30th ed., Carolyn A. Fischer and Carol A. Schwartz, eds, New York: Gale Research Inc., 1955). The Girl Scouts organization promotes an ethical, moral and affirmative code of conduct through its Promise and its Law. These have changed slightly over the years, but as of today the Girl Scout Promise is: "On my honor, I will try to serve God and my country, to help people at all times, and to live by the Girl Scout Law." This Law states: "I will do my best to be honest, to be fair, to help where I am needed, to be cheerful, to be friendly and considerate, to be a sister to every Girl Scout, to respect authority, to use resources wisely, to protect and improve the world around me, to show respect for myself and others through my words and actions." Jesse Stuart would certainly applaud these ideals as they echo his own words in the Preface to *The Thread That Runs So True*.

Today the Girl Scouts of America has over three and a half million members, and millions more of America's women have been involved in and influenced by the organization. Juliette Low began the Girl Scouts of America in response to Sir Robert Baden-Powell's founding of the Boy Scouts in England to teach young men to be resourceful and self-reliant. From the start of Sir Baden-Powell's organization, girls were interested in a similar group, and his sister, Agnes Baden-Powell, was influential in the organization of the English Girl Guides, a forerunner to the Girl Scouts of America. In 1911 in Glen Lyon, Scotland, Juliette Low, with seven girls, set up her first troop of Girl Guides. She also established troops in London, England in that year, but in 1912 she sailed to her native America with the dream of founding an American counterpart to the English Girl Guides. She devoted the rest of her life, her tireless energy and her financial capital to the establishment of this valuable American institution. This book traces her life from her girlhood in Savannah, Georgia during the Civil War, through her happy but childless marriage and her commitment to the founding of the Girl Scouts, to her death in 1927. As with many great undertakings, her dream was not easy to realize, but through her dedication and inspiration, she left a great legacy to American girls and women.

Danny L. Miller

ACKNOWLEDGMENTS

Preparation of this book could never have been accomplished without the help of many people in whose hearts still lives the memory of Juliette Low. To members of Mrs. Low's family I am deeply indebted, not only for the great amount of time they so graciously gave me, but for the use of family letters, records, photographs, and especially Juliette Low's own diaries and letters written from childhood until her death. I owe a special debt of gratitude to Mrs. Samuel C. Lawrence, Mrs. Low's niece and namesake, for the days of time she gave me and the large amount of tedious work she did in copying old family letters and documents for my use. These dated back to Civil War days and were of particular value in giving the early chapters of the book color and authenticity.

Greatly appreciated, too, is the tremendous help I received from the Girl Scouts organization. Women who had worked in the Scouts with Mrs. Low willingly shared their memories and experiences. Others who had come into the organization after her death assisted greatly in gathering of factual material and in checking the manuscript for accuracy of detail.

To the many people who so willingly cooperated in making this book possible, my sincere thanks.

Mildred Mastin Pace

One

A General Comes To Call

Every day the sound of the guns came closer, closer, until now the house shook with the firing. General Sherman and his Yankee army were just outside Savannah, and there was little hope that the Southern army could stop them. The streets were already filled with people in flight--women and children and old people, in carriages and wagons, on horseback, on foot.

Inside the house the mother bound a ribbon around the littlest girl's hair and said to the two children, "Now you may go out in the back yard and play under the big tree. Nellie, take Daisy's hand. I'll call you when it's time for your supper."

The boughs of the pittosporum tree spread low, its heavy leaves making a cool, green tent. Under the tree the guns seemed farther away than they had in the house, the fighting more remote. For the war had changed the house. Silver and crystal had been hidden away. Coats of black paint disguised the shining brass door plates. The house had become somber, but the tree remained the same.

From the slave quarters beyond the yard, a small playmate, Hetty, came running to join the children under the tree. They climbed among the low branches, swinging from them and dropping themselves gently to the ground. When they tired of this, the children pretended that each large branch was a room, and the tree a house where they entertained imaginary guests, and everything was very fine indeed, for the war was over, father was home, and there was plenty of food to eat.

Daisy put an abrupt stop to the game by asking her sister, "Nellie, what do you think General Sherman looks like?"

"Oh, Daisy, you shouldn't say his name so loud!" She frowned, thought a minute, then answered in a whisper, "Like--a devil." She pushed the picture from her mind. But Daisy enjoyed the picture and dwelt on the idea with relish. Imagine! Seeing a man who looked like a devil! Aloud she said, "We will see him. Right this minute he isn't far away!"

Hetty drew farther back into the darkness of the tree, away from such talk.

Nellie said sternly, "No! We will never see him. Mama will take us away before the Yankee army comes."

"She won't either. She's not afraid. And neither am I!" Daisy's dark eyes flashed, "I'm a Southerner! I'm not scared of old Yankee Sherman."

"You'd better stop saying such things. Anyhow, I think Mama called--I hear Grannie's voice." The two sisters ran into the house.

They stopped short of the sitting-room threshold, hearing their grandmother say, "But you must leave--it isn't safe for you or the children. Women and children have been ordered to leave."

"I won't leave until I see Willie. No one can order me to go!"

Daisy looked at her older sister with an "I-told-you-so" air. Mama wouldn't go until she had seen Papa. The two little girls walked slowly into the sitting room unnoticed.

The older woman said softly, "Nell, if I know my son, Willie would want nothing more than to know you and the children are safe up North with your people. Besides, Willie is behind the lines fighting. How would you find him, even if you got through the lines?"

"I'd find him," the younger woman spoke with quiet determination. "And I won't leave until I've seen him. Until I've seen him with my own two eyes and know he is alive and well, I cannot go North. I must see him."

The grandmother looked at her daughter-in-law with despair. "You know, some people are already talking--saying you aren't afraid to stay because you're a Northerner . . . that Sherman will help you because your own are fighting on the Yankee side."

"I know they are talking," she said angrily. "Two of our charming neighbors came this morning, scared and whining, asking me to intercede for their protection when Sherman enters the city!"

"Oh, no! What shameful behavior! What did you say?"

"I told them to get out! I told them I had no notion of asking favors of Sherman for my own--if they wished protection from the Yankee general they would have to beg it themselves."

Daisy stood straight and proud beside her mother, her dark eyes as bright with anger as her mother's were. The mother drew the child to her, and when she spoke again her voice was gentle. "It doesn't matter what they say. My own people may be fighting for the North, but my husband is a Southerner, fighting for the South. And that is where my heart is. As soon as I see him, we will go."

The grandmother sighed. She knew the spirit of this Northern woman her son had married. She had made her decision and argument clearly was a waste of time.

The guns were so close now that even in the solidly built Gordon home glassware trembled on the shelves and pans rattled in the kitchen. The slaves who had stayed on went about their work silently, with bewilderment born of uncertainty. They lowered their voices, softened their steps and waited for the Yankee army.

Early one morning Daisy was wakened by her nurse who wrapped her in a blanket and carried her out onto the balcony. She was so sleepy, it was difficult to rub her eyes open.

"Why are you waking me, Mormer? I'm so sleepy--"

"To see a sight, a real sight--look!"

Daisy could hear the music now, and the heavy tramp of marching. She looked down at the endless columns of blue uniforms marching past, thousands and thousands of Yankees--the first the child had ever seen--marching past her home, through the streets of Savannah.

The whole household was up now, and over the thud of the marching feet Daisy could hear her baby sister, Alice, crying, her mother's soft voice soothing her.

As the day wore on it was filled with rumors and rumors of rumors. It was said that all women and children were to be sent out of the city at once. It was said that the plague was spreading. On everyone's tongue were the words, "Have you heard . . ." or

"They say . . . ."

In the Gordon home the children and the slaves became tense and excited, wondering what to expect. Grandmother Gordon fretted more and more because the family had remained. But the young mother, as she moved about the house on her routine of duties, behaved as if the Yankees had never marched through Savannah, as if the streets of the city weren't flooded with the blue uniforms, as if Sherman were a thousand miles away.

The following day, she called the entire household together and quietly announced that General Sherman had sent word that he wished to call. She would receive him that afternoon. That was all.

Daisy shivered with excitement. At last she was to see Sherman! And right in her own home. The two little girls waited in a state of high suspense until time for the caller to arrive.

In stiffly starched dresses, with fresh ribbons in their light-brown hair, they were taken into the sitting room by their nurse.

Daisy was shocked to see that General Sherman looked like a man--just an ordinary man, and a skinny one at that--not a devil at all. And there was her mother, talking to him as calmly as if he were any other gentleman caller. But her head was held high, her voice cool and polite--she would ask no favors of him!

Sherman said, "Very well; if that is how you feel--but when you leave the city, Mrs. Gordon, I will see, of course, that you have safe conduct. . . ." He stopped speaking, seeing the children.

Mrs. Gordon said, "General Sherman, these are my daughters, Eleanor and Juliette." Daisy caught her breath when Mama spoke the name. For, while her real name was Juliette, she was always called Daisy. Oh, Mama was being very formal.

The General smiled at the children, and, holding out a hand to Daisy, drew her up into his lap. At this gesture, Daisy saw a startled look cross her sister's face, but Daisy was not the least perturbed. In fact, the entire situation was unexpected and filled with interest. What's more, she was quite close now to a Yankee soldier who stood near Sherman. This soldier was a very strange man, for he had but one arm.

The General took a little packet from his pocket and gave it to the child. "Open it carefully or it will spill," he warned her. "Open it and taste it."

Inside the packet were tiny white grains. They tasted something like molasses in that they were sweet. But the flavor was different. Daisy liked it. Nellie came over now, looked at the white grains and took a pinch to taste.

"It's sugar," the General smiled at them. It was the first Daisy had ever tasted.

Daisy was still fascinated by the man with only one arm. When she could bear it no longer--and having been emboldened by her position on the General's lap--she asked, "Where is your arm?"

"Got it shot off by a rebel," the man answered.

"Very likely my father did it," Daisy said matter-of-factly. "He shot lots of Yankees."

There was a horrified silence in the room, and the mother's face was no longer calm. In a choking voice she said to the nurse, "Take the children away, Mormer." And Daisy knew that her meeting with the General had ended in disgrace.

The exodus from Savannah was greater now than it had ever been before. Getting out of the city became increasingly difficult. Roads were filled with troop movements, and the trains leaving the city were filled with soldiers. Over the same roads sick and wounded were being brought into the city. Dead were being carted away. The women and children, obeying orders to leave, found travel difficult indeed.

"Are we going too? When are we going?" the children asked. The grandmother worried. The mother was silent.

But one day she came into the grandmother's room where the children were listening to a story. Her eyes were shining, her voice full of relief.

"I have it," she said, holding up an envelope, "permission to go through the lines and see Willie! He's been notified that I have the order. I'm sure a meeting place will be arranged, and he'll be waiting--" She hugged each of the little girls and said, "As soon as I get back we'll leave. We'll go to Chicago to Mama's people, where there are no guns and where there is plenty to eat. Won't that be fine?"

They saw her off, confident and gallant, all smiles. Grannie was worried and dubious. But if Nell had to make this journey before she could leave Savannah, it was best for her to go and have the trip done with.

She came back a few days later, satisfied and ready to prepare for the trip north.

"He's well, and in far better spirits that I thought to find him. A trifle thin," she reported, "and worried about us because the journey will be hard. He's afraid, too, it may be bad to take the children north in the wintertime. Bless him!" She looked at the children with deep affection. "Your father is a wonderful man," she said, "a man of great courage and loyalty. Even while fighting a war, he is more concerned for our safety than for his own."

$\mathcal{T}wo$

NEW WORLD IN CHICAGO

The trip to Chicago was never-to-be-forgotten! With Savannah in a state of siege, the only practical way to leave the city seemed to be by water. So on a small, overcrowded boat the young mother and the three children sailed from Savannah to Hilton Head, South Carolina. There they boarded a larger steamer and sailed up the coast to New York. The larger ship, too, was overcrowded, and food was scarce. It was January, and as the ship headed north it became too cold for people to go out on deck. Inside the air was thick and stuffy. Almost everyone on board, except Daisy, was seasick.

When they reached New York at long last, Mother's brother, Uncle George, was there to meet them.

If the little girls felt a bit shy with this strange young uncle, they soon got over it. He tossed them up in the air, making them squeal with excitement and delight. He rode Baby Alice on his shoulder and teased her into outbursts of laughter. He brought warm clothes for them all, and a velvet cloak for his sister.

"It's old, Nell--but, as Mama says, there is always an elegance about velvet."

Laughing, the young mother wrapped the cloak about her. "It is elegant, George, and very warm. It was good of you to carry it."

With Uncle George, they all forgot the dreadful boat trip that was behind them, and for the moment the long, tedious railroad journey that lay ahead.

The trip West by rail was dirty and slow. No matter how tightly they kept the windows shut, the children were covered with cinders. There were frequent changes, and long waits in cold stations. Meals were irregular and the food was not very good. When the family reached Chicago, they were weary to the point of exhaustion.

But it was a joyful reunion at the Kinzie home!

Some of the grownups worried because the children were so thin. But Grandmother Kinzie said, "Well, they do look thin--and pasty, now. But they're bright-eyed and intelligent, and nothing is wrong that some nourishing meals won't cure. We'll soon have them fixed up."

"Food was short," the young mother answered. "We had to go without many things. I did the best I could--and I think I managed better than many."

"I'm sure you did," the grandmother smiled at the children.

And how they did eat! Grandmother Kinzie had a never-ending supply of plump roasting chickens, baked hams, thick cream to go on apple dumplings, fat loaves of bread fresh from the oven, jars of fruit preserves, bowls of sweet butter. There was food the children had never tasted or had forgotten.

Chicago was a new world to the little girls. The house they lived in was different from the house in Savannah. Because of the cold Chicago winters, there were not the wide, spacious rooms with high ceilings and many windows of the South. The rooms were small and cozy, low-ceilinged, and shut off against drafts.

When they looked out the small squares of windows, they saw bare trees and ground covered with snow--the first snow they had ever seen. And when they went outdoors, the first intense cold they had ever felt nipped at their cheeks and numbed their ankles.

Indoors, the stories they heard were new ones, too. Their favorite story was the true one their grandmother told, the story of a little girl who had been kidnaped by Indians. The little girl was Grandmother's own mother--the children's great-grandmother. When

Grandmother was a little girl she had sat many, many times and listened to her mother tell the story, fascinated just as Daisy and Nell, and every other child who ever heard the story, were fascinated by it.

"Tell us again about Eleanor Lytle and the Indians," the children would beg. And, once more, Grandmother would tell the story.

* * * *

It was a bright October afternoon in 1779, and Eleanor, who was nine, and her brother, two years younger than she, had found a new game to play. Some huge trees had been felled back of their father's house and the children were having great fun climbing among the branches, racing each other to the "top" of the tree. The house was on the Plum River, in western Pennsylvania, wild, beautiful country, with many Indians still living on the land. The children were quite used to Indians, and all they had known were friendly.

But suddenly Eleanor stopped the game and whispered in alarm, "I saw an Indian--a strange one."

"Where?"

"Over there." Though they both looked in the direction of her pointing, they could see no Indian. If he were friendly, why should he hide?

In alarm the children ran into the house. But their mother was not frightened. Indeed, she scolded them for being such babies.

"You know you have never seen unfriendly Indians in these parts! Have you forgotten the moccasins left you only last week by your good friend of the Shawanoes? Now go back to your play. Your father would be ashamed to know you are so easily frightened."

So the children went back to the trees and their new game. A few minutes later they heard the low call of a quail in the woods behind them. Was it a quail? Or was it a signal? They stopped their playing.

Listen! Again the low, soft call.

"I hear the rustling of branches in the woods," Eleanor whispered.

Before her brother could reply, they were seized from behind. Dark hands covered their mouths, and their frightened eyes looked up into the faces of strange Indians.

Muffled so they could not cry out, the children were swiftly led through the woods, along narrow rough trails. All through the afternoon the Indians hurried them, removing the strips of cloth that silenced them only after they had gone deep into the wilderness. The children stumbled along in terror, for they had heard many terrible stories about children captured by hostile Indians.

Toward nightfall they were so exhausted--their fright had increased with their fatigue--that they could no longer pretend to be courageous. They began to sob, softly at first, then uncontrollably. The Indians had been rough and harsh with them all afternoon. But now their distress seemed to touch one of the men. One Indian came over and tried to comfort them, telling them in sign language that they would not be harmed. He pulled long grass and made a pallet for them to lie down on, and shared his dried meat and corn with them.

Just as they were feeling a little less distressed, another party of Indians arrived. To the children's horror, they saw that their mother had been taken by these Indians. In her arms she carried their three-month-old baby brother. Her eyes told the children to be quiet, and she gave them a brief half-smile of reassurance. In a way, her presence helped them to be brave. But now they were frightened not only for themselves but for their mother and the baby.

In sign language and a few words of half-English, the Indians questioned Mrs. Lytle.

Where was her husband?

She explained that her husband had been away all day helping with a house-raising.

Where were the other little boy and girl?

The mother said she hoped they had escaped. She had been taken so completely by surprise there had not been time to warn the other children. She had no idea where they were.

These explanations seemed to satisfy the Indians, and the poor worn-out woman and her tired children were allowed a short night's rest.

Early the next day the hard journey was resumed. The mother, carrying her young baby, tried valiantly to keep up with the swift steps of the Indians. The baby became heavier and heavier in her arms. Her footsteps slowed as the day wore on.

Finally one of the older Indian men took the baby from her arms. Mrs. Lytle hoped he was being kind, relieving her briefly of the precious burden that had become so heavy. But her fears mounted as she saw the Indian linger farther and farther behind the party. She knew any sign of fear, any outcry, might endanger the lives of all of them. So, stoically, she hurried on.

After a while, the Indian and the baby disappeared. Mrs. Lytle watched anxiously for him to return to the party. In a short while he reappeared, his arms empty. The young mother knew then that he had murdered her baby and left the little body behind in the woods. Though her grief was almost more than she could bear, she realized the lives of her other two children, and indeed her own life, depended on her self-control. With tremendous courage, she permitted herself no sign of grief and hastened her footsteps. Her fear now was that the children would tire and lag behind, or in some way break under the terrible strain.

After many days of this painful travel, the party reached a Seneca village on the headwaters of the Allegheny River. Here they were met by the chief of the tribe, an Indian known as Big-White-Man because he had a slight strain of white ancestry. He took the captives to the main lodge where his mother, widow of the head chief, and known as The Queen, resided.

Singling out Eleanor, Big-White-Man presented her to his mother saying, "My mother, I bring you a child to take the place of my brother who was killed by the Lenape six months ago. She shall dwell in my lodge and be to me a sister." Then he added, "Take the white woman and her children and treat them kindly. Our father will give us many horses and guns to buy them back again."

Mrs. Lytle now understood what the Indians wanted. They meant to keep Eleanor, to bring her up as an Indian child to replace one they had lost! As for herself and her son, they were to be held for ransom. By "our father" Mrs. Lytle knew the chief meant Colonel Johnson, who lived at Fort Niagara and who would most certainly see that whatever heavy ransom the Indians demanded would be paid for the return of her and her son.

But what had happened at the Lytle home while the mother and her children were making the long journey to the Seneca village?

Mr. Lytle arrived home from the house-raising in the evening of the tragic day. No one ran to greet him. His shouts when he entered the house were answered by echoes. There was no living person anywhere around. Frantically he hurried to the nearest neighbors, who lived quite a distance away. The neighbors could tell him nothing. But hurriedly they prepared to join the search.

All night they combed the woods, finding no clues. In the morning as they approached an old hut they were startled to see a boy and a girl standing on a high bank. Yes, they were two of his children--six-year-old Thomas, and little Maggie, who was only four.

"What happened?" Mr. Lytle cried, running to them. "Where are your mother and the other children?"

They did not know what had happened to their mother and the baby, to their brother and sister. But this is what happened to them.

They were playing in the garden when they saw strange Indians steal into the yard and creep toward the house. The boy realized their only chance of escape was to get as far away as possible, while the Indians were in the house. Quickly he helped his little sister across a fence where they were hidden by the thick growth of a wild berry patch.

"We must go along as fast as we can," he whispered.

But the little girl was barefoot, and before they had gone far the briars cut her feet. Her brother took off his shoes and stockings and put them on her. This did not help much, because the shoes were far too big and kept sliding off. Soon the stockings were torn to shreds and her feet were bleeding.

Now the little girl began to whimper and say she could go no farther.

Thomas knew their safety lay in distance. He said calmly, "Then Maggie, I must kill you. For I cannot let you be killed by the Indians."

The younger child pleaded, "No, no, Thomas. Don't kill me. I don't think the Indians can find us now. I must stop!"

"Yes, the Indians will find us if we stop. And I could kill you so much easier than they would."

The brother even pretended to be looking for a stick with which to kill her when the little one refused to move. Finally she promised she would go on with no more complaining, and they started out again.

After a while the children came out into a field where cows were grazing. With wisdom far beyond his six years the boy said, "I know these are Granny

Meyers' cows. We will hide here now until sunset. Then the cows will go home and we will follow them. That will surely take us to Granny Meyers' place, and we won't be lost."

This the children did. But to their dismay Granny Meyers's hut was deserted. However, they hid there, frightened and hungry, until morning when their father found them standing, in bewilderment, outside the doorway.

Leaving the two children with neighbors, Mr. Lytle lost no time in going to Fort Pitt for help. There a detachment of soldiers was assigned to him to help in the search. The men searched the forests for days and made cautious inquiries of everyone they met. Finally they came to the Seneca village, and learned they had reached the end of their hunt.

Now Mr. Lytle entered into a treaty with the Indians for the ransoming of the captives. It was not too difficult to arrange for the freedom of Mrs. Lytle and the boy.

But when it came to Eleanor, nothing they promised--no amount of property, horses, guns or money--could budge the Chief in his decision to keep the girl as an adopted member of the tribe.

"She is my sister," the Chief said. "I have taken her for my mother, to supply the place of my brother who was killed by the enemy. She is dear to me, and I will not part with her."

When at long last the father and mother realized that it was impossible to take Eleanor with them, they told her a sorrowful farewell, bade her be brave and obedient, and promised to continue their efforts for her release. Though they were thankful that three of their children had escaped the Indians, the Lytles' return home was a very sad one. Their youngest murdered, their eldest held captive by a tribe of the Senecas!

After her parents and brother left her, Eleanor was in the deepest despair. The Indians tried to be kind to her, to interest her in their games, their feasts. But nothing they did consoled her for the loss of her family and her home.

However, Eleanor was a nine-year-old with a great deal of energy, an intelligent child who had always been interested in everything that went on about her. She watched the activities of the Indians, and gradually she began to take part in them. As she made friends among the Senecas her heartache for her own people lessened. Slowly the memory of her own home faded. The Indians were delighted at how quickly she learned their language, adopted their customs. She moved with such speed and energy, they named her "Little-Ship-Under-Full-Sail."

For four years she lived this life, and her family's

hope for her release grew dimmer. Then, in 1783, with peace restored between Great Britain and the United States, there was a general pacification of the Indian tribes. The Lytles began once more to hope for the return of their child, who was now almost fourteen.

With the hopes rekindled, the Lytles left their home and moved to Fort Niagara, near which the great Council Fire of the Senecas was soon to take place. Colonel Johnson agreed to enter into negotiations once more with the Chief, and this time to go in person to Big-White-Man.

Colonel Johnson arrived at the village during the Feast of the Green Corn. Everyone was in festive dress. His eyes quickly picked out the white girl--her garments covered with silver brooches, innumerable strings of white and purple wampum around her neck, colored beads twined in her hair, her deerskin moccasins lavishly embroidered with porcupine quills. It was evident, indeed, that the Chief considered her his sister.

The Colonel had long been friendly with the Seneca tribe, and he was received cordially. He saw, too, that the festival had made the Indians more generous than usual, kinder and warm-hearted. It was a good time to take the Chief aside and tell him the reason for his visit.

The father and mother of the girl, he explained,

had moved their family hundreds of miles to Fort Niagara, giving up their home in the forlorn hope that they might have a glimpse of their daughter. Would the Chief not let them just look upon her? Her parents loved her deeply--would the Chief not permit them one, only one, brief meeting with their child?

The Chief's heart softened as he listened to Colonel Johnson. At last he promised to bring his adopted sister to the Grand Council at Fort Niagara. There he would let the white parents see the girl.

But this was to be done on one condition. The Chief must have the Colonel's oath that there would be no attempt to reclaim the girl, and that no proposal would be made to him to part with her. This promise the Colonel made.

The Chief had "Little-Ship's" word that she would never leave him without permission. He knew he could trust her. Besides, he believed that she was happy living with his tribe, that she had forgotten her own parents and had no desire to leave. So he had no fear of losing his adopted sister when he took her to the Grand Council.

The mother and father stood on the bank of the river and watched bands of Indian chiefs and warriors gathering on the other side. The agreement was that when their daughter and Big-White-Man arrived, boats were to be sent across for them and the brief reunion would be held there on the river bank in the presence of the Chief.

At long last the Lytles saw the party they had been watching for emerge from the woods and join the other bands at the Council Fire. Immediately the boats were off. And in a matter of minutes, the father and mother saw their daughter coming closer, closer, standing in the boat, the Chief holding her by the hand.

The boat touched the shallows. Someone hauled it up on the bank. The Chief dropped the girl's hand, and with a cry she was in her mother's arms.

In surprise and dismay the Chief watched the scene of deep affection. He reached out his hand, as if to draw the girl back. But as he saw her cling more tightly to her mother, sadly he turned and stepped into the boat.

"She shall go," he said. "The mother must have her daughter again. I will return alone."

He crossed the river, and in spite of the protests of the other chiefs, mounted his horse and turned toward home. He was too broken-hearted to remain at the Council.

Big-White-Man never saw his adopted sister again.

Although Mr. Lytle did not think the Chief would fail to keep his word, there was an undercurrent of fear that the Senecas might try to restore the white girl to their saddened Chief. So, in a few weeks, the family moved again--for the last time--across Lake Erie, near Detroit. There Eleanor soon became adjusted to the happy life of her own family, and before long it scarcely seemed that she had been away. But she never forgot Big-White-Man and the many Indian friends she made during her four years with the Senecas.

*   *   *   *

When Grandmother finished the story, the children were silent for a while.

Then Nellie said, "I have the same name, Eleanor, haven't I, Grandmother?" And Daisy, not to be outdone, said quickly, "I have two names--Juliette, my real name, and Daisy."

Grandmother smiled, "As a matter of fact, I think you should have three names, Daisy. You are very much like your great-grandmother was when she was a little girl. I think we should call you 'Little-Ship-Under-Full-Sail.'"

This delighted Daisy, and throughout her life when any of the family called her "Little Ship," the name brought a quick smile.

In the house in Chicago, Grandfather had stories to tell, too. He was the U.S. Government's paymaster for the Indians, and had known the Indian people all his life.

Because he paid the Indians in silver, they called him "Shaw-nee-aw-kee," or "Silver Man." They admired Mr. Kinzie. For one thing he was a skillful player of their difficult game, La Crosse. In foot races he had beaten the fastest runners of the Menomenees and Winnebagoes. He could speak more than thirteen Indian languages, and was the first white man to master the language of the Winnebagoes. So the Indians came to the Kinzie house not only for the silver due them, but for the help and advice from the white man they respected.

In clear weather, Grandfather received them out-of-doors, in the yard. The children, peeking out the window or from behind a tree, would watch with deep interest. The Indians behaved with great dignity and deliberation. A meeting with their grandfather was full of long silences, and Grandfather always waited patiently until each Indian had had his say before he himself spoke.

The first time Daisy witnessed one of the councils she whispered to Nellie. "What is wrong with Grandfather? He just sits there."

"Shhh!" Nellie hushed her.

"But why doesn't he say something, Nell?"

"I don't know. Watch." So they watched, silent themselves, and learned how one did business with Indians.

These were not the only delights of the new home. To Daisy's pleasure, there were animals to play with, too. A big gentle dog, a mother cat and a family of kittens, cows and horses in the barn. But best of all, there was Grandmother Kinzie's parrot, which followed the children about scolding for crackers and attention. It was a rich blue-pearl gray with a scarlet tail. Daisy thought it the most beautiful creature she had ever seen.

The war now seemed very far away to the little girls, and the grown people did not communicate their anxieties to them. They wanted their father, of course. But when they spoke of it, their mother--never letting them know of her own deep need of him--cheerfully assured them that soon the family would all be together. . . . So, for a time, life went pleasantly by in Chicago.

Then, suddenly, overnight, life in the Kinzie home turned into a nightmare of worry and fear.

Three

TROUBLED TIMES

The sitting room was cold and dark but for the chill gray of early morning at the windows. The young mother shivered as she groped her way across the room toward the hearth. The fire was laid, ready. She touched a match to it and fanned the first feeble burst of flame.

The stair door opened and Grandmother Kinzie came in, lamp in hand. Over her night clothes she wore a heavy woolen robe, and a shawl was drawn over her head.

"What's wrong, Nellie? My, it's cold," she shuddered. "What are you doing up at this hour?"

"Daisy's ill," the mother's voice trembled with worry. "I think we'd better send one of the hired men for the doctor."

Grandmother Kinzie set down the lamp and walked over to her daughter.

"Are you sure it is so serious, dear? You know, sickness that strikes in the night is very frightening. Sometimes by daylight we find we have worried needlessly."

"That is true. But the child has a high fever--I've been up with her for several hours now, and I'm afraid she is getting worse, not better."

"Well, in that case, we must get the doctor. As quickly as possible."

By the time the doctor came, Daisy was delirious. He examined the child and shook his head in despair. "It is brain fever--she is dangerously ill."

In the days that followed the shadow of death lay over the household. Each evening the young mother, sitting beside the child, wondered if she could possibly pull through one more night. Each morning as she bathed the hot, fever-wasted little body and listened to the weak, delirious murmurings, she wondered if the miracle of life could last through one more day.

There was also the fear for the other children. Where had Daisy caught it? Would Nellie catch it? And baby Alice?

Now the house had the strange hush of a house where someone lies desperately ill. The children saw the grave figure of the doctor come and go, heard the murmured consultations of the grownups. Mama they saw fleetingly, as she went in and out of the sickroom, closing the door swiftly and silently behind her. It seemed to them that everyone walked on tiptoe, spoke in whispers. Even when Grandma Kinzie told them stories, her voice was low.

Fortunately the other two children stayed strong and well. And gradually the faces of the grownups brightened a bit.

"She has held her own so far," the doctor said. "It's a good sign."

Little by little the fever subsided, the breathing became more even, the pulse stronger. At last came the day when the doctor said confidently, "She is out of danger now." Then he added, "But the child has had a very severe illness, and for a time after her recovery, you must not cross her, she must have her own way."

Mama sighed. "Oh, dear, I'm afraid I'll have a very spoiled little girl if we must follow that order."

Nellie laughed, "No you won't, Mama. Daisy's always had her own way. She's that kind of a person."

Everybody laughed. Partly because Nellie was right and partly because the long weeks of suspense were over and it was fine to be able to laugh again.

Once more life in Chicago was happy. Only the fact that the war continued and father was still away from them and in danger kept those days from being perfect.

Spring came--a spring such as the children had never seen. Everything seemed to wake up at once. One day the bitter cold ended, the ground became soft beneath their feet, and there was a sweet-moist fragrance in the air. Soon the bare trees put out fragile green, and the first wild flowers opened like stars against the dark earth.

Grandmother showed the children where the hepatica grew in the woods, where to find the spring beauties and the adder's tongue. The cherry trees bloomed, and the apples were in bud.

First came the message that Lee had surrendered at Appomattox. This meant the war's end.

"Will we see Papa now?" the children asked. "When is he coming?"

Six days after the good news came tragic word of President Lincoln's assassination. This filled the Kinzie men with dark doubts for the nation's future, and the children's elders discussed it at great length in solemn voices.

It was several weeks more before the family had news of father. The day his letter was received was one of real thanksgiving in the Kinzie home. The message was read and re-read, and for the first time in a long, long while Mama was really happy.

Father was not only safe, but as soon as he could arrange it, he was coming to Chicago to take them home.

Grandmother Kinzie said, "We will miss you and the children dreadfully, Nell. And I am afraid the South will be a poor place to live for the next several years. I don't suppose Will would ever consent to settling here?"

Mother smiled, "No. Will's roots are deep in the South. His people, our home, what may be left of his business, are there. We must go back."

It was late summer before father was able to reach Chicago. The reunion of the family was a happy and exciting event. At first he seemed a little strange to the children, for they could not remember ever having seen him out of uniform. But he was quite as handsome in his new salt-and-pepper suit, maintaining--as he always would, and always did--a military bearing, the straight fine figure of an officer.

There was so much to talk about, so much to tell, even bedtimes were forgotten and the children stayed up long after the lamps were lighted, listening.

The day after his arrival, William Gordon took his young wife aside and said, "Nellie, the war has completely ruined my cotton business."

"I was prepared for that," she answered.

"I'm afraid we are going to be poor--for a while."

Nellie Gordon smiled a sad little smile, and said, "All of the South is going to be poor for a while, Willie. I've known all along that we would go back to rebuilding."

They stood, silent and thoughtful for a moment, then Mrs. Gordon said briskly, "Willie--I've made up my mind. I'm going to sell my Chicago lots. You'll never refinance your business without capital!"

"No, I don't want you to do that, Nell--your father gave you those lake-front lots for your own."

"Of course he did. And I'll use them for my own. I can't think of anything on earth better to use them for than to help my husband with his business." She looked at him with bright, wise eyes. "It's a good time to sell, Will. I can get a good price for them now. I would have had to sacrifice them earlier."

"Yes," he agreed, "it is a good time to sell. Only--"

So Mama sold the Chicago lots.

Now began the exciting business of getting packed and ready to go. There were elaborate preparations to be made for the long trip back with the three small children.

Finally the farewell visits to the Kinzie relatives had been made, to all the friends and neighbors. Daisy said a special goodbye to each of the animals that had been her friends--the big gentle dog, the mother cat and her newest litter of kittens, the cows and horses in the barn.

Watching her, Grandmother Kinzie said, "Nell, I've never seen a child so fond of animals."

"She's been that way since she was a baby," the

mother smiled. "It nearly broke her heart when, as food became scarce, we couldn't keep all the dogs and cats. Her father is the same way, you know."

But for Daisy the hardest farewell of all was the parrot--the big gray parrot that followed her around and scolded for food. She thought seriously of asking Grandmother if she could take him along. But then, Grannie did love the parrot. And he might not like Savannah. Sighing, she gave the bird a last tidbit, as her mother called, "The carriage is here, children."

So, on a bright September day, the Gordons left the North to return to Savannah.

It was good to be back home, in Savannah, the family together. But the homecoming was troubled, too. For the war had left the South sick and worn, crippled. Unlike the North, the people of the South had largely depended on agriculture for their living. Cotton--requiring large acreage and lots of labor--was their chief crop, their main source of prosperity.

Now, in the South, the fields were seared. Rich pastures had been turned into battlefields, crops burned, cattle slaughtered. Even much of the land that had been untouched by battle had grown to weeds and undergrowth while the men were off to war. Farms that had depended on slave labor found themselves without help during the war years because many of the slaves ran away. And while the women of the

South had shown the greatest courage--often working the fields themselves--they could not do everything. As it was, they had woven their own homespun for garments when cloth became scarce, struggled to feed and house their families, and had even helped to supply the Confederate army. Now, the war over, the South was worn out.

In Washington, Congress believed the South should be punished. If President Lincoln had not been assassinated, perhaps the defeated states would have been treated more gently. Lincoln had said that once the war was over, everyone would have to work together for a sound reconstruction program. But Andrew Johnson, who succeeded Lincoln, could not convince Congress that this plan was the wise one to adopt.

The Southern people had maintained their hope and courage through the darkest days of fighting. But now came the bitterest days of all. There was little money, almost no production. Food, scarce during the war, continued to be scarce. Taxes rose sharply and many of the people had nothing with which to pay them. They saw their land sold to strangers-- often men from the North--who bought it for a song.

And what of the people who had been their slaves? They were bewildered and confused. They were free, but free to do what? Well, for one thing, they could now vote. In many cases the men from the North told them how to vote. And it was, of course, the way the Northerners wanted the election to go, not the way the Southerners wished.

This was the South to which Daisy and her family returned.

Understandably, most of the Southern people were very bitter toward the North. But in the Gordon home, the father--though he had been an officer in the South-ern army and wounded in battle by Northern guns--spoke of tolerance.

"Our only hope," he said, "is to work toward an understanding between the North and the South. There has already been too much hatred, too much bitter-ness. It will accomplish nothing."

Daisy could still say to herself, fiercely, "I'm a rebel!" But even as she spoke the words, she remem-bered the kind people she had known in the North and the months she had spent there. Her father, she knew, was right.

The buildings behind the Gordon home, where the slaves had lived, were almost empty. Although a few of the slaves stayed on as servants on a wage basis, most of them had gone--some to work on plan-tations, others no one knew where.

Daisy no longer awakened in the morning to find the kind face of "Mormer" smiling down at her. And little dark Hetty no longer shared the shade of the pittosporum tree with the children.

Mother hired a young girl with yellow hair and blue eyes, a girl who had been born across the sea, to help with the work and the care of the children.

The Gordons--as father predicted--had little money. To make matters worse, on their return to Savannah they found that many of the needed and useful things in the house had disappeared. Almost all the pots and pans had been stolen. Dishes and kitchenware were gone. These--and other things--had to be replaced.

With so little hired help in the home, the children became more and more self-reliant. Nellie helped Daisy with tasks that were too difficult for the young child, and both of them took a hand in helping with Alice.

In the spring there was a new baby.

Much to everyone's joy, this fourth child was a boy. He was named William for his father, but the children called him Baby Willie. He had fiery red hair and, so Mama said, a disposition to match the hair. His sisters thought he was the most wonderful baby in the world.

The fall after Willie was born, it was decided that Daisy was old enough to go to school. Daisy was to learn to read from the book that Nellie had used, "Little Tales for Very Little Children."

Daisy tried hard to concentrate and be good. But it was quite difficult for her to sit still and keep her mind on her lessons. The stories themselves she thought were a little silly. "The Cat and the Hen," "Sam and His Dog!" So she would think of more exciting things, until Mam'selle Lucile or Mam'selle Marguerite, her teachers, called her back to her lessons.

School did one wonderful thing for Daisy. In school she learned she could draw! She could draw better than any of the other children--even better than children much older than herself. The trouble was she could draw only when her teacher gave her permission. Try as she might, she would forget, and when she was supposed to be copying words from her books or writing down numbers, she would neglect these for the more fascinating task of drawing a picture. Then there would be a gentle scolding from the Mam'selles, and reluctantly Daisy would turn to school work. Poor Daisy! She did not realize it then, but all through her school days this talent that gave her so much joy was also to bring her woe!

$\mathcal{F}our$

SUMMER AT THE CLIFFS

Mama smiled at the three little girls and said, "I declare, I think each of you grew taller during the two months you were gone--and you're brown as berries!"

"We should be," Eleanor exclaimed; "we were hardly ever indoors, except to sleep."

"And eat," Daisy added.

"I learned to swim," Alice announced. "And I can swim almost as fast as Daisy. . . ."

"Listen, Mama. . . ."

Suddenly all three children were talking at once. Mama said, "Go wash, now, and put on fresh clothes, then you can tell me all about it."

The girls had spent the summer at Etowah Cliffs, their Aunt Eliza's home in northern Georgia, and Mama knew there would be lots to tell. There was no place on earth more fun for children. The long rambling house, with more rooms than a child cared to count, was built along the cliffs that rose from the Etowah River. From its double piazzas one could look down to the river and across half a mile or more to the shoals. Often there were as many as twenty children there at once--and always room for more. With so many playmates, and so many wonderful places to play, the children had much to do. Back of the house were the rose gardens, then the orchards, and beyond the orchards came the woods--mile after mile of pine woods, dark, cool, exciting. With trees to hide behind, shadows to conceal them, the children were Indian tribes on the warpath, or the Confederate army routing the Yankees. They could yell at the tops of their voices, make all the noise they wanted, and nobody was disturbed. When they wearied of running, jumping, hiding and chasing, they dropped down on the pine-needle carpets and told stories, or hushed and listened to the sounds in the woods. Then there were the shoals. There the water was shallow at the edge, sloping gradually to depth. Even the smallest cousin could wade and splash in safety, while the other children, by walking out a short distance, had excellent swimming.

But most exciting of all were the cliffs. These the children could climb until, it seemed, they reached dizzy heights, the fun of climbing intensified by a small feeling of danger. The highest point was Termination Rock. From the edge of the rock the children could look down, down, down, far down to the river below.

"Mama, see what I have!" The children were back again, full of excitement. Daisy held up a white garment trimmed with different colored ribbons. "It was my costume in one of our plays--I was the Spirit of the Rainbow--and I couldn't bear to leave it behind, so Aunt Eliza let me have it."

"I was in the play, too," Alice said. "I was Little Bertie, and Eleanor was a witch. It was so good we charged admission."

"We made sixty-five cents, and sent it to the Indian missionaries."

"Daisy was the star actress," Eleanor said. "Oh, Mama, you should have seen her play Mary Queen of Scots! I was the executioner, and when I chopped off her head I spilled pokeberry juice to make it look real--it was wonderful!"

"But it's awfully hard to get out of your hair," Daisy remembered, then changing the subject said, "Mama, Alice insisted on hanging over the most dangerous part of Termination Rock. She wouldn't mind me, nor Nellie. She was unmanageable!"

"You can't order me about!" Alice said tartly. "Even if you are older. You tattle on me and I'll tell Mama how you mimicked Aunt Eliza's friend from Cartersville. . . ."

"When I did, you shrieked with laughter," Daisy

retorted.

"Children, children!" Mama hushed them. "Now what's this I hear about Alice learning to swim?"

"I did! I can swim faster than any of the other children my age."

"She can, Mama, for a fact! I helped teach her," Daisy said. "But I want to tell you what the Stiles boys have at the Cliffs--two donkeys, and two darling little Angora goats and a cart. Oh, do you suppose I could have an Angora goat for my own? I want one so much. You could give it to me for a combined birthday and Christmas gift and I wouldn't ask for anything else!"

Mama laughed. "Well, we already have quite a few pets, Daisy. I don't know about adding a goat to the collection. . . ."

"Tell her about the snake, Daisy," Eleanor interrupted. "Daisy met a snake when she was all alone in the woods!"

"This big," Daisy said, spreading her arms as far as they would reach. "Maybe even bigger. The snake stared at me, and I just stared back at him. Pretty soon he went away. I wasn't a bit afraid."

"That's one way to get rid of a snake," Mama chuckled.

Then suddenly the conversation took another turn. "Oh, you haven't seen the literary magazine we published!" Eleanor cried, and ran to get copies.

"We put out an issue each month, and now that we're gone, Caroline Stiles is going to keep on with it, and we're to send her contributions," Daisy explained. "It was so much fun--we each took the name of a flower so nobody could be sure who the authors were."

"Except you," Alice added. "You kept your name, Daisy, and everybody could tell what was yours."

"Daisy was the chief contributor, too," Eleanor said, returning with the papers. "She not only did most of the drawings, but she was the best one of all at verse."

Mama took the sheets from Eleanor and looked at them carefully. "I think this is excellent! Daisy, these drawings are very good. . . . Alice, you and Nellie will have to tell me your noms de plume so I can admire your work too." She stopped suddenly at a verse titled, "The Piggy," and read half-aloud,

"I was passing by a pig-sty
When I heard a piggy say,
'I would like to live in rubbish,
Forever and a day.' . . .

"Daisy! What a sentiment to put in verse!"

The children rocked with laughter, "Oh, Mama, read it all. Daisy wrote it because our governesses had given us nothing to read but the most sanctimonious stories--every one ending with a moral. We were so sick of them. . . ."

"I wrote it in protest," Daisy laughed; "read it all, Mama--it has a moral at the end too."

But Mama glanced at the clock and jumped up, putting the papers aside. "Gracious, I had no idea it was so late. Your father will be home. I'll read it after supper, and you can finish telling us about your summer then. Papa will want to know what you did, too."

So, each summer when the children came back from the Cliffs, there were new adventures to boast of, fresh experiences to relate.

When young brother Bill grew older, he went too, of course. Later there were two more children--Mabel and another red-haired baby brother, Arthur. In due time they also made the Cliffs summer headquarters.

The lessons they learned in those months of freedom and activity, the wealth of fun they had, were never forgotten. Long after she was grown, Daisy would slip off to Etowah Cliffs, when she had a chance, for a visit with Aunt Eliza, a walk through the deep pine woods, a swim at the shoals.

Five

GROWING UP

Even with the capital provided by the sale of the Chicago lots, rebuilding his business in Savannah was up-hill work for Mr. Gordon. Little by little, year by year, it strengthened, however. And gradually the feeling of "hard times" slipped away from the Gordon home.

As time went on, faded floor coverings were replaced with new carpets. Worn draperies came down, new damask went up. A large downstairs room that had--much to Mrs. Gordon's distress--been used as a storeroom during and just after the war, was properly converted into a library. The house began to take on some measure of the graciousness and beauty that belonged to it.

Meanwhile Daisy, growing older, was consumed with a new desire. She wanted to go to boarding school. Nell had been allowed to go away to school the previous year. Mam'selle Lucile and Mam'selle Marguerite were as nice as they could be, prim and proper and thorough in their teaching.

"But," Daisy complained, "I'm getting too big for that little school. Let me go back with Nell for the fall term. After all, I'm almost fourteen!"

"But you're so little," her mother worried. She had not forgotten the illness that had left Daisy weak and frail for so long a time, and it was difficult for her to send the child to strangers.

"Mama, please don't call me little. You know I hate it. I may be small for my age--but I'm strong." She looked shrewdly at her mother for a moment. "You know, Mama, you're not very big yourself. Maybe I take after you."

Mama laughed and gathered the child into her arms. "Maybe you do--poor darling. We'll talk school over with Papa and see."

So, one day early in September, the Gordon household was filled with the confusion of leave-taking.

Their trunks were already gone, but the two girls were still remembering odds and ends--a length of ribbon, Nellie's new needlecase, a sketch book--to cram into the already overflowing valises.

Dressed in new silk plaids, with matching bonnets, the two sisters were filled with grownup importance. Daisy wished they weren't to be accompanied by a governess. She felt entirely adequate to make the journey with Nellie, and no grownups. But Staunton, Virginia, was quite a distance, and Mama considered it quite out of the question for them to make the trip alone.

Soon the coach would be brought around to the front door, and they would be off. Daisy dashed upstairs once more to say goodbye to her baby brother, Arthur. Even in the excitement of going away to school she found it hard to leave him.

"Mama," she said for the tenth time, "please do promise to write and tell me everything Arthur says or does."

"I'll try, Daisy. And you--wear your braces every day, hear me? I don't want you growing up stoop-shouldered."

Father had advice too. "Pay strict attention to your lessons, Daisy. Don't permit your drawing to inter-fere. I do hope they are able to teach you to spell at Stuart Hall."

So the last bits of advice filled in the final tense moments of waiting. Then there was the coach and the flurry of affectionate goodbyes. For a second, as the house disappeared from sight and the horses went faster toward the station, Daisy wanted to turn back. With a rush of pure love she thought of the other four children, Mama and Papa, how could she ever live without them?

Nellie said comfortably, "Mama says she'll send us things for our room when we tell her what we want. We'll fix the nicest room at Stuart Hall, won't we, Daisy?"

"Oh, yes," Daisy breathed the words. How lucky she was to have a darling sister like Nellie to room with at school! She vowed she would never, never quarrel with Nell again! She would always be kind and sweet to her and let Nell have her own way. She would always be grateful for this sister. . . .

The girls did fix up their room--quite elegantly, they thought. And gradually they made new friends.

But there came a night when Daisy lay on the narrow bed in the pitch dark of their little room and knew that she could no longer keep from crying. She had never known such loneliness could exist. If she could have only one glimpse of her mother, or hear her father's voice, or stand for one second in the warmly lighted sitting room at home, she would be all right. The need for her family started as a little knot of misery and had grown to such enormous proportions it seemed to fill her completely with a choking ache. And now to make matters worse--there was the demerit. She tried to stifle her sobs in the pillow. Finally she could bear the loneliness no longer--though it was against the rules to speak after the lights were out--she whispered across the darkness to Nell. "Nell, I got another demerit."

"Oh, Daisy!" Nell--also against the rules--was out of her bed and in with her sister. "Whatever for?"

"Drawing in French class."

"Again?"

"Oh, I can't help it, Nell. I mean so to be good and not disgrace Mama and Papa," she choked as she spoke the names. "But the class is so dull--and before I know it, I'm drawing. It infuriates Miss B."

"Shhh, stop crying," Nell comforted her. "The trouble is, you learn things so quickly--you have time left over."

"No, it's not that, Nell. I forget to behave. I'm so miserable."

"Well," Nell said practically, "it's done now. And you'll never get to sleep crying and brooding over it. Let's think about something pleasant."

"What?" asked Daisy, in a tone that inferred there was nothing pleasant to think of.

"Well--the masquerade!"

"Oh, let's. Nell, I'm going to fool everybody this time. Last time you know I went as Little Boy Blue, and everybody knew me, because I'm the smallest girl in the school. But this time--I'll tell you. You won't tell a soul, will you? You wouldn't give me away?"

"Of course not! Whisper lower," Nell warned her.

"I'm making a false face with a tall pasteboard box, and on top of this I'll wear a hat. It will make me look ever so much taller. And I'm going to stuff myself with pillows. I don't believe a soul will know me: do you?"

Nell muffled her giggles in a corner of the quilt. "No, I don't believe anybody will in that get-up. . . . Now, I must get back into my own bed before we both get demerits."

At the masquerade it was quite a while before anyone guessed that the fat man with the tall hat and funny painted-on face was Daisy. Oh, the masquerade was quite a success, and the chief subject of conversation for days. For there was very little play time at Stuart Hall. Rules were strict. For long periods at a time the girls were allowed to speak only French or German--no English. If they forgot and lapsed into their native tongue, they were punished. Strict attention was demanded at all times in classes. And the girls were expected always to behave properly as young ladies should.

All in all, life at Stuart Hall was quite rigid.

After Daisy had spent two years there, her parents decided to send her to another boarding school where she would have subjects a little more advanced. Nellie, now, had gone to New York to attend a French finishing school. So when Daisy changed schools, it was her younger sister, Alice, who accompanied her.

The new school was Edge Hill. It was also in Virginia, near Charlottesville.

Edge Hill was very strict, too. But there were many more things to do, and consequently more fun.

"Oh, Alice," Daisy exclaimed shortly after their arrival, "do you know there are horses here! If Papa says we can afford it, we can go horseback riding!"

To make life even more exciting at Edge Hill, there were clubs. Two of them: Theta Tau and Theta Psi. Daisy joined the Taus. Her greatest immediate problem then became how to scrape together the necessary money with which to buy a gold club badge. Unfortunately, just as Stuart Hall had not done much to help Daisy's spelling, neither had it managed to improve her arithmetic. No matter how she tried, her accounts never added up properly, her allowance never quite stretched to meet all the expenses she had planned for.

At home Mama said, "Daisy is growing up. She has become so exacting about her clothes. Look here. A detailed drawing of how she wants her new dress made. And a sample of the kind of braid she wants it trimmed with!"

"She is growing up," Papa smiled. "I realized it sharply when she wrote asking if she could spend Christmas with the Hunters in Washington. I wouldn't be surprised if her cousin hasn't written her hinting at dances and parties and some fine young men."

"Oh, dear, she does seem young for that! But--she is just sixteen. I suppose we should let her go--only Alice must go, too."

That Christmas in Washington was one of the gayest times Daisy had ever known! There were parties and dances, as Papa knew there would be. And young men from Harvard, cadets from West Point. Daisy was surprised, when her first shyness wore off, to find how at ease she was with these young admirers.

To really top the visit off, Daisy and her cousin Minnie, without asking, ordered the family's best carriage, the driver in livery, and went calling. Daisy had never felt so grand in her life!

Alice scolded. "You're trying to act grown up! What would Mama and Papa say?"

"Don't be so indignant!" Daisy said with great superiority. "After all--you're just a child. I shall write Mama and Papa about it in detail!"

When Daisy went to Washington, most of the Christmas gifts she took with her she had made herself. Among them was a picture, a water color, she painted for her Aunt and Uncle. Daisy's drawing teacher, Miss Belle, had thought the girl not advanced enough to work in color, but Daisy had begged so hard, she finally consented. When she saw the picture she said, "Daisy, I am delighted. You show real skill in your use of water colors." She was thoughtful for a moment, then added, "When you come back after Christmas, I think I will let you try working on porcelain with oils."

Daisy rushed back to her room to tell Alice the good news. "The only trouble is, oils are frightfully expensive. Do you think Papa can afford them?"

"Write and ask him," Alice answered; "I think so. He afforded us the horseback riding."

Shortly after Christmas vacation was over, Daisy received the extra money for her oils, and began working in the new medium with great enthusiasm and pleasure.

Her joy in her art work would have been complete had she been allowed to draw and paint what she saw, instead of copying and being restricted to exercises.

Sometimes, when she had an unsupervised hour in the afternoon, she would slip off to the nearby woods with her sketch pad or a piece of modeling clay. How she wished the birds and squirrels, the quick little chipmunks, would stay still long enough for her to capture them on paper! Once she was surprised and delighted to see a little fox a farm hand had tamed. Half scared and quiet, it crouched until her quick pencil sketched it.

Occasionally Alice or a schoolmate would consent to pose for her. But she found this tedious. And besides, Daisy was usually dissatisfied with her work and destroyed the drawing or clay model, so they did not even have "a work of art" to show for their trouble.

At Edge Hill, as at the previous school, Daisy found it difficult to obey all the strict rules. In exasperation she finally admitted, "I'll keep clear of the big scrapes. But I can't avoid the little ones!"

A box of food would come from home--then she could not resist having girls in after the lights were out, to huddle in the darkness and eat the sweets that were so much sweeter because they were being consumed against the rules. Or to slip down to the floor below with another girl--a floor empty except for the room in which the one-eyed French teacher lived--and tell ghost stories in the darkness. Such a session always brightened a dull period. But, alas, usually she was caught.

Then there were teachers with long faces, scoldings, quotings from the Bible, readings from the Prayer Book, until, as Daisy confessed to Alice, "I'd rather they'd swear at me for an hour or punish me in any other way! Nothing is worse than all that righteous indignation."

"You dread it so," Alice said, "I'd think you'd try to behave and avoid such scenes."

"I do try, Alice; really I do," Daisy answered miserably. "Oh, dear, sometimes I think this place should be called 'Edge of Hell' instead of Edge Hill."

In spite of her difficulties, when the school year was finished, Daisy was awarded the Drawing Medal. This was one of the highest honors a student could achieve. Daisy was proud to receive it. But she was troubled, too. Would her father think she had given too much attention to her art?

But no, "Your marks are all good, Daisy. You've done very well indeed," he praised her.

"Papa, I still can't spell," she lamented. "And I try hard to use the dictionary. But even that doesn't help me. For example, when I wrote last I wanted to be sure and have it perfect. And I couldn't spell choral. I looked under c-o, I looked under k-o, and then Alice told me it is spelled c-h, of all things!"

Papa smiled, shaking his head. "I don't believe you'll ever learn to spell in English. Perhaps you can spell in French." He was silent for a moment, and Daisy waited, knowing he had something serious to say. "Your Mama and I have decided to send you to New York next year. To the Mlles. Charbonniers' school, where your sister Eleanor finished. Would you like that?"

Like it! Daisy remembered, with a rush, all the things Nellie had written about--theaters, the opera, dancing classes, the shops on Fifth Avenue. Daisy had supposed, since Nellie had gone to the Charbs, as she called them, someday Papa would send her there too. But always when it crossed her mind it was something in the future. Suddenly it was something for now! Well, almost now.

"Oh, I'd love it, Papa," she said. Then added, with a note of surprise in her voice, "Why, Papa, I've grown up!"

Six

BOARDING SCHOOL IN NEW YORK

When Daisy left for the Mlles. Charbonniers' it was the first time in her life that she had been without a sister. Nell was to stay home and make her debut in Savannah. Alice was thought too young for the New York school and returned to Edge Hill.

The parting with her sisters was somewhat eased because Mama was going with her to New York to see that she was safely entered in the French school on East 36th Street. But her mother left after a very brief visit, and Daisy was alone.

Well, not quite alone. She had two roommates, which was fine. But, in order to see that the three girls behaved, there was also a governess in the room. Daisy called her, behind her back, an old "renard"--and while the woman probably did keep Daisy from breaking rules, the old "fox" also spoiled their fun.

Rules here, too, were very strict. And at first Daisy

wished bitterly she could leave New York and go back to friendly Edge Hill, where Alice was.

The girls had to rise at six A.M.--though breakfast was not served until eight. One hour was allowed for dressing and putting their rooms in order. The hour between seven and eight they had to devote to study.

"How can I study when I'm starving to death?" fumed Daisy, who was always hungry.

After breakfast, and until twelve o'clock lunch, they were in classes. The curriculum was heavy, and except for German twice a week, all classes were in French. They studied Histoire Romaine, Histoire Fransaise, Histoire du Moyen Age, Literature Fransaise et Anglaise, grammaire, verbe et analyse, composition et poésie, traduction, lexicologie.

The afternoons were more interesting. Three days a week Daisy studied drawing. However, the teacher was very fussy, and kept her doing perspective for the first several months--drawing combinations of blocks and lines, when she wanted, more than anything, to draw what she saw, to splash color across paper and see forms take shape.

But when Daisy complained, the teacher said severely, "You are not ready for color yet. Soon I may let you work in light and shade. Oils? After Christmas, perhaps." Then, again, Daisy would think about dear old Edge Hill, and she would wonder how she ever could have misbehaved at the school where, so it seemed now, everybody had been so kind; how she could ever have been so ungrateful as to nickname it "Edge of Hell."

Twice a week she studied singing. Daisy loved music, but she dreaded the singing lessons.

The teacher used what he called "the new method." And as one of Daisy's roommates, Nannie Brigham, teased, "With your voice, Daisy, I think he would have to use a new method."

The singing lessons had one great compensation. Since it would not be proper for a young lady to be alone in the room with a gentleman--even her singing teacher--one of the other girls had to accompany her as "chaperone." When the lessons were over, they walked daringly back to the Mlles. Charbonniers' on Fifth Avenue. The Charbonniers did not approve of Fifth Avenue, and when the girls were taken out for walks by the teachers--walking two by two and only for the exercise--they weren't allowed to use Fifth. It was much too lively, too crowded with smartly dressed ladies and dashing young men at whom, the French spinsters said, "the young ladies stared." So they walked on Madison Avenue instead--this being considered much more conservative.

Daisy hoped the Charbs would never ask them what route they took back from the singing lessons!

It was along Fifth Avenue, late one afternoon, that Daisy met and bowed to a young gentleman she knew. Nannie Brigham was with her, so after making proper introductions the three started sedately up Fifth Avenue toward 36th Street. Suddenly Daisy remembered that the Charbs would consider her behavior highly improper--on any street.

With great dignity she addressed the young man, "Mr. Drummond, if I say something rude to you, you must excuse me. As far as I am concerned, I am very glad of your company. But the Mlles. Charbonnier would not, I am sure, like me to walk on the street with a young gentleman."

Mr. Drummond apologized, and explaining that he did not know the rules of the school, bowed and left them.

After he had gone, Nannie turned to Daisy in admiration, "My, you were very sophisticated, Daisy. I'm sure he thinks you are quite a grown-up young lady!"

Daisy smiled smugly, then said in a worried voice, "Oh, dear. I hope nobody saw us! Wouldn't the Charbs have a fit!"

But nobody had seen them, and the walks continued. Sometimes, much to Daisy's disappointment, the singing teacher would keep her overtime and the girls would have to go back on horsecars to avoid being scolded for tardiness. Dinner was served promptly at 5:30, and lateness was not excused.

After dinner the girls were sent to the study hall where they worked in silence until time for bed. They escaped study hall only on nights that where assigned to sewing, and on certain Tuesday evenings when, for a brief period, all the girls and the Mlles. Charbonnier gathered in the parlor, and callers were permitted.

This was always a very stiff occasion. Once Daisy tried to make a Tuesday evening a bit festive by wearing her elegant black silk dress. For this she was roundly scolded by the Charbs and told, "Never wear your black silk except on Sunday."

The routine was so rigid, letters could be written only on certain days.

But there were bright occasions too. Sometimes the girls were taken to the theater, usually to a matinee. And once in a great while they went to the Opera. Daisy loved these occasions, her only complaint being that, "The Charbs get seats so far up and so far back, the people on the stage look like the size of darning needles."

Among her greatest joys were the dancing lessons. Every Saturday morning, Daisy and five other girls from the school went to Dodsworth's Dancing Academy.

Mr. Dodsworth was tall and serious, his wife small but quite as dignified. Each lesson began with the

Dodsworths standing at one end of the ballroom and, dressed in formal evening clothes, receiving the pupils. Each pupil, upon arriving, was expected to walk the full length of the room and make a bow to the Dodsworths before taking a seat along the wall. This procedure always seemed slightly ridiculous to Daisy, and it was only with difficulty that she managed to keep a perfectly straight face. Once she failed! One of the girls from the Charbs, a friend of Daisy's, had been complimented by Mr. Dodsworth on the low and graceful curtsey she made. The next Saturday Daisy's friend was determined to do even better. She bowed so low she fell flat on the floor. Daisy tried not to let a giggle escape--but she did not succeed. The Dodsworths looked at her in consternation. It was difficult indeed to know who was the most disgraced--the girl who fell or Daisy who giggled!

At the Dodsworths' the lessons on how to enter a room, how to curtsey, how to sit properly in a ballroom, with one's feet in a graceful position (but never crossed) and one's skirt arranged in classical folds--these Daisy considered things she must learn as quickly as possible and be done with. What she waited for was the moment when the music started and the actual dancing lessons began. Then Daisy loved every minute of it.

But when one of her roommates asked her, "What do you like best about school, Daisy?" her answer was prompt, "Painting--it is my greatest joy!"

Her teacher quickly recognized that he had a talented pupil. Not many months after she began her lessons, she was painting in oils. And by spring--to Daisy's great joy--she was allowed to paint from a real model.

"I guess an artist wouldn't consider her a very good model," Daisy said to her friend when she announced the happy news. "She's about fourteen, and the poor little thing is really very homely except for her yellow hair. But she's alive!"

Through the school year there was also an occasional fun weekend. Daisy had cousins in Newark, Trenton, and other places near New York, where the young people gathered for sleigh rides in the winter, teas and dances, lawn parties in the spring. And Daisy was always welcome.

All in all, the first year at the Charbs was a very happy one. When it was over, Daisy found herself looking forward to returning the following year.

She joined her family for the summer at a resort in West Virginia and was delighted to find that Mama and Papa planned to send Alice to the Mlles. Charbonniers' in the fall. Daisy would have a sister with her again!

The only trouble was, Alice did not want to go. She begged her parents to let her stay with them, or return to Edge Hill where she felt at home. New York, the French School, held no interest for her. But Mama and Papa both thought that Alice should be schooled in French, that she should have the advantage of spending at least one year in New York.

Daisy, eager to have her sister with her, told and retold the things they would do, the fun they would have. Reluctantly Alice went to New York.

Several weeks after school started, Alice became ill. At first it was thought to be a cold, something from which she would shortly recover. But as the fever rose, anxiety mounted. When the doctor said, "It is scarlet fever," the Charbonniers sent for Mama.

Christmas came, and the Gordons scarcely marked its coming. Alice lay burning with fever, delirious and incoherent. Doctors stood by helpless. For the second time Mama kept a day-and-night vigil at the bedside of a child near death.

On December 30th Alice died.

This was the first great sorrow in Daisy's life. It was intensified because she had urged her younger sister to come to New York where she contracted the disease. It was intensified for her parents because they had insisted on sending Alice away. Gentle Alice, who wanted more than anything else to stay home with them.

Daisy went back to school, after Alice's death, in

utter desolation. And the shadow that lay over the house she left was a very deep one.

But all the Gordons were people of strength and courage. The mourning must be set aside. Alice would live always in their hearts and memories, and she would live there, not as someone to weep for but as the girl they had all loved in life. Sometimes, in later years, when the five other children had married and moved away, it seemed to Mama and Papa that Alice was the one who had stayed.

Seven

THE HANDSOMEST MAN IN SAVANNAH

Daisy set the dozen plates side by side on the table. "Do you like them Mama? Do you think I painted them well?"

"They are exquisite, Daisy. You painted them beautifully. Some of the work is so fine. I don't see how you did it with a brush."

Daisy beamed with happiness. "The more fine work you put on, the better. But it is tedious!"

"Now that your school days are finished, Daisy, I think you should make your debut in Savannah."

"Oh, Mama. I knew you were going to bring that up. Must I make my debut? I dread it!"

"Nonsense. You'll have a merry time. Just as Eleanor did."

"Well--please ask Papa if first I can have some time in New York to study china painting."

So early fall found Daisy in New York. It was

even gayer now than before. For Eleanor had married one of the Parker cousins, and Daisy had a sister living in Newark.

Back in Savannah, Mama finished reading Daisy's latest letter aloud. Papa said, "I don't know how much studying Daisy is doing--but she certainly seems to be having a fine time. Do you suppose she will want to come home?"

"Of course. She will be home in November as planned," Mama smiled. "You know, Will, I don't believe there is a place in the world where a young girl can have as much fun as right here in Savannah!"

In Savannah a girl made her bow to society when she attended her first Cotillion Club ball. So, on a winter evening, Daisy sat in the drawing room of the Gordon house and waited nervously for the young gentleman who was to take her to her first Cotillion.

"What will I do if nobody asks me to dance, Mama? Oh, I'll die, really I will!"

Mama glanced up from the embroidery she was working on, "Never mind. You'll be asked to dance."

"And if you aren't, unfortunately you won't die," her red-headed brother Bill teased her. "You'll just sit there, a miserable wallflower."

"Oh, Bill, stop!" Daisy wailed. "I couldn't bear it--"

Mabel spoke quickly, "You'll be the most popular girl there, Daisy. You look beautiful. And wasn't it

79

sweet of Grannie to lend you her pearl bracelet!"

Daisy fingered the bracelet. It lent her some assurance. She rearranged the folds of her white gown--it was a lovely dress! And the velvet slipper bag Mama had embroidered for her was a real beauty.

Then--there was the doorbell. Her escort was announced. And Daisy left, chattering gaily to cover up her uneasiness.

Reaching the hall, each girl went into the dressing room to replace her walking shoes with the dancing slippers she carried in her velvet bag. When all the girls who were to be presented were ready, the chaperones proceeded to the ballroom. Then Daisy and the others joined their escorts and in a formal line the young people were received by Savannah Society.

This ordeal over, the orchestra struck up a waltz and the dance was on!

The minute the music started, all of Daisy's qualms melted. She found herself in demand for every dance, and between dances she was always the center of a happy and admiring group.

At home, late that night, tired but happy, she said, "Oh, Mama, I had a wonderful time. I love parties!"

"Of course you do--you always have," Mama laughed.

"I was afraid I wouldn't have as jolly a time at grownup parties, as I've had with boys and girls. But now I know I will!"

It was a winter filled with parties and dances, regattas on the river, boat races, balls at the Yacht Club.

"We always have fun at a gathering if Daisy is there," her friends said. It was true. She was witty and brilliant. She loved people, and she loved to see them have a good time. Moreover, whatever she did, she did well, so that whether the event was a dance, an amateur theatrical, an evening of games, or a boating party, Daisy contributed a large share toward its success.

Oh, there were plenty of boyfriends for Daisy! But there was one whom people called "the handsomest man in Savannah." Secretly, Daisy thought he was the handsomest man in the world. His name was William Mackay Low. He had shining blonde hair and the bluest eyes Daisy had ever seen. She was feminine enough to know, too, that her own dark loveliness was set off by Willie Low's fairness.

His father was English, but Willie's mother had come from Savannah, and the Lows owned one of the most beautiful old homes in the city. Though Willie had been born and reared in England, his family made frequent trips to the United States.

Willie's father was in the cotton business, and had extensive interests in this country as well as abroad.

Now his father was sending him back to Savannah to see to the Low's cotton business there. So, instead of the brief visit he usually made, young Mr. Low probably would remain in Savannah for some time.

As a matter of fact, he had returned to the States in the fall, while Daisy was in New York, just before she went home to make her debut. Willie had called on Daisy in New York and, much to her delight, presented her with a little black-and-white fox terrier, brought all the way from England.

"A gift from my sisters, Jessie and Mary," he said.

Daisy wondered. Was it from Jessie and Mary-- or had Willie, knowing how she loved animals, brought it himself? She wanted to believe the latter. But then, perhaps it wasn't proper for a young gentleman to give a young lady a dog. She didn't know. However that might be, the puppy was a darling! She named him Ko-Ko, and took him with her everywhere she went. Now, in Savannah, Ko-Ko was an important member of the household and shared Daisy's affections with Nox, her black kitten.

When the exciting winter ended, Mama and Papa decided it was time for Daisy to have the advantages of travel in Europe. She was to sail from New York in June. Before Daisy left Savannah, Willie Low said to her, "You must visit my family in Warwickshire while you are in England. My mother and sisters will be disappointed if you don't."

So, on that first, exciting, memorable trip abroad, Daisy did spend some time with the Lows on their beautiful estate in Warwickshire. Renewing ties with the family increased her interest in Willie.

When she returned to Savannah, she resumed the lively life of parties and cotillions. But more and more she was seen with Willie, less with her many other admirers.

Papa--watching Daisy come and go, always happy and full of plans--decided Mama was right: young people in Savannah had a very fine time.

Then, abruptly, the gaiety and fun ended for Daisy. She waked one Sunday morning with an earache. Mama was away--in Newark with Eleanor who was expecting her first baby.

"I won't bother Papa," Daisy said to herself. "I'll go on to church as usual, and on the way home I'll see the doctor and have him give me that new treatment I heard about in New York."

Daisy's doctor listened as she described the treatment. "I'm sorry, Miss Gordon, but I never heard of putting silver nitrate in the ear."

"It's being used successfully in New York," Daisy said. "You do have silver nitrate, don't you?"

"Yes. But I don't know how much to use, nor what strength."

"Well, use your own judgment as to the amount and strength. But please hurry. If you won't do it for me, I'll go to another doctor who will."

Daisy was so insistent that the doctor finally injected the silver nitrate. Almost at once Daisy found herself nearly out of her mind with pain. She did not want the doctor to know how intense the pain was. Somehow she managed to get out of his office without his realizing. And, with great difficulty, she walked the short distance home. As soon as she was indoors, she collapsed.

This was the beginning of a long and serious illness. When she finally recovered, they found that she was partially deaf in the ear that had been treated.

"There is an ear specialist in Baltimore . . ." someone would say, and Daisy would be taken to Baltimore. "There is a man in New York . . . a doctor in Boston . . . a chap in Atlanta. . . ." Wherever her parents heard of a specialist who might help, there Daisy went. But the answer was always the same, "The silver nitrate destroyed the tissues. As far as we know, nothing can be done."

"She looks so thin and sickly," Mama worried. "Maybe if she were stronger physically it would help. Perhaps she needs a change."

So Daisy was sent north for a round of visits with friends and relatives. She returned to Savannah in fine spirits and good health. But the deafness remained.

It was after her return that she and Willie confessed they had been secretly engaged for almost two years. Now they wanted their families to know. Papa wrote Mr. Low and received a pleased letter back, assuring him that Willie would have a share in the Low business and stating that he wished to give the children the Savannah home for a wedding gift.

Happy, her head full of plans, Daisy said, "I want to be married on Mama's and Papa's wedding anniversary--December 21st--and I want a white wedding."

Eight

A White Wedding

Daisy looked up from the drawing board, removed the paper she had been working on, and handed it to Willie. "How do you like that design for the bridesmaids' brooches?"

"Very much," Willie answered. "The daisy design is most appropriate, and we can have the wedding date carved along the stem."

"That's just what the stem there is for," Daisy laughed.

Willie took a small package from his pocket and handed it to Daisy. She opened it carefully and cried, "Oh, how beautiful! Come look--" she called the family, "Willie has the diamonds for the brooches."

Since boyhood Willie had been interested in stones. He had made a study of them through the years, until he was an expert at judging gems. When it was decided that his gift to each of the six bridesmaids was to be a brooch, he took great pleasure in choosing the stones carefully.

But with even greater care he had chosen another set of diamonds. These he did not show Daisy. He had combed the diamond markets until he had a collection of stones, each perfect, and all perfectly matched. These he was having set in a crescent and a star--his gift to his bride.

"What kind of flowers are you going to have, Daisy?" Mama asked.

Daisy's eyes softened as she answered, "I want lilies of the valley, Mama--they were Alice's favorite flower."

The months before the wedding were very busy ones for Daisy. Not only was Willie's father making the young people a gift of the Savannah home, but he was having it all redecorated and refurnished to their taste. So, in addition to the wedding plans, there were new furnishings to buy, painting and papering to be supervised. Daisy loved every bit of it--but she was busy from morning till night.

Hers was a church wedding, held at noon. In her white gown, carrying the corsage of white lilies of the valley, wearing no ornaments except the exquisite jewels Willie had given her, Daisy was a lovely bride.

The six bridesmaids were all dressed in white and alike, their gowns of fine chiffon, embroidered in white, little white chiffon hats on their heads. Each, of course, wore her diamond brooch.

A wedding breakfast at the Gordon home followed the ceremony. Daisy thought her home--the home she was about to leave--had never looked lovelier. Hearth fires burned in every room, casting a glow of warmth and light. The pale winter sunlight shone through the high windows and caught in the crystal chandeliers. Flowers were everywhere.

After she had tossed her wedding bouquet from the wide staircase and changed into traveling clothes, Daisy and Willie dashed for the carriage in a shower of rice. For their honeymoon they were to have an island all to themselves, Saint Catherine's Island, not far from Savannah, lent to them by a friend.

Shortly after they reached the island, Daisy realized with dismay that the ear that had troubled her before was starting to ache. She was determined to say nothing about it to Willie. Finally the pain became unbearable and she could hide it no longer. Worried and distressed, Willie insisted that they go back to Savannah and see her doctor.

The doctor examined the ear and found that a grain of rice lodged in it had caused an infection.

The cause of the trouble removed, the pain gradually diminished. But when it was all over, Daisy realized that she was entirely deaf in that ear. And there was no cure.

In spite of her ear trouble, the winter in Savannah was a very happy one. Establishing her new household, doing her first entertaining as Mrs. William Low, Daisy was a busy and happy bride.

When summer came, the Low's cotton interests needed Willie back in England. So, closing up the beautiful Savannah house and saying farewell for the time to her family and friends, Daisy left her own country to take up a new life with her handsome young husband in England.

Daisy went to England at the peak of the Victorian era--a period when people of wealth made an art of leisure. The society in which Willie Low moved was dominated by the Prince of Wales, and it was a life of sumptuous parties in vast mansions, of hunting meets, costume balls, dinners of great elegance.

Daisy and Willie arrived in England just in time for the colorful Naval Review given in honor of Queen Victoria's Jubilee. This was Daisy's introduction to the brilliant social life she was to be a part of for some years to come. From the time she boarded the beautifully decorated yacht that morning until the last rockets flung their ribbons of light across the skies that night, she found it brimful of excitement and color.

At the end of the day she said to Willie, "I never dreamed I would ever meet so many famous people.

Nor did I know there were so many Dukes and Duchesses, Lords and Ladies in all of England!"

"You will meet royalty, Daisy. Before you can really be a member of London Society you must be presented at Court."

As Daisy said later, "Being presented at Court is no bed of roses."

First there was the matter of a gown--it must be splendid, but not showy, with a train exactly six yards long. Gloves must be white and three plumes must be worn in the hair.

Daisy's dress was white satin, little festoons of ostrich feathers stitched on the skirt, and a filmy overskirt of white silk tulle. Willie had given her a set of diamond swallows, and these she wore in flight across the white bodice of her gown. Diamond stars were pinned on a slender band of feather trimming that crossed from shoulder to waist.

"Just look, Willie," she cried in delight after she dressed, "the diamonds you gave me glitter through the feathers like the Milky Way! Oh, I am elegant!"

She turned around in admiration to look at the train. It was white silk with white satin brocade embroidery, and lined with pink to give a touch of color to the gown. Then there was the tulle veil, the three plumes in her hair, and her bouquet of white flowers.

Daisy was only one of many being presented to Queen Victoria that day, and she arrived at Buckingham Palace to find, much to her surprise, a mad scramble instead of the dignified scene she had expected!

As she described the whole thing later, "Really, Willie, I felt more as if I were in Billingsgate Fish Market than Buckingham Palace." She laughed, "Such pushing and rushing, and scrambling for places! Everyone, of course, wanted to get in first and have the ordeal over! Oh, they were all very sorry to crowd and push, and apologized continually. But it took quite a bit of doing to keep my clothes on my back and my feet on the floor!"

The "ordeal" started at three in the afternoon, and it took Daisy until six that evening to go through the seven rooms that led to the throne room.

"I was so tired! But I didn't dare sit down or stop to rest, or I would have lost ground. My train grew so heavy--and the bouquet! By four o'clock I was sure it weighed a ton." Her eyes twinkled, "But I solved that problem. The lady in front of me had a gown with a large bustle. I just set my bouquet down on her bustle and she carried it for me the lengths of all the rooms--never knowing what a service she rendered in a time of great need."

"But you did finally see the Queen?"

"Oh, dear no," Daisy laughed. "By the time I reached the throne room, the poor Queen had long since become tired and gone to her rooms. But there was plenty Royalty left--Princess Christine and her husband, the Duchesses of Albany and of Teck, two young princesses, and the oldest son of the Prince of Wales were all there. I made my curtsey before each of them--and I felt exactly as if I were bowing to figures in Madame Tussaud's wax museum. Really, I almost expected to see ropes of red silk around them and a sign reading, 'Please do not handle the figures.'"

Having made her formal entrance into London Society, Daisy soon took her place as one of the most popular young hostesses. The Lows became celebrated for their hospitality.

One of the most famous cooks in Europe presided in their kitchen. In addition, however, when Daisy left the States she took her cook, Mosianna, with her. "I'll get hungry for Southern cooking, I know I will," she said. "And Papa, you must promise to send me all the good American things I can't get in London."

From the United States to Daisy's kitchens went food then strange to England--country hams and sausage, brandied peaches, canvasback ducks, cans of rich terrapin soup, fat turkeys, fresh green peppers, peanuts, maple syrup, and sweet potatoes. Papa even found a way of wrapping corn on the cob so it kept

on the long journey. Daisy's famous cook had cooked for kings! But Mosianna had to teach her what to do with rice and sweet potatoes, how to cook the country hams and make waffles.

The food served at the Low's was the talk of London. So popular did some of the dishes become, a fashionable Piccadilly food shop had to import some of the items to keep its customers happy.

When they were first married, Daisy and Willie rented a country estate, waiting to buy until they found the very one they wanted.

They had been married almost three years when they bought Wellesbourne. It was situated in Warwickshire, in Central England, a country of wide meadows, green valleys and winding rivers.

Proudly, Willie took Daisy over the whole great house, every acre of ground. As they walked through the rooms--room after room after room--Daisy said, "Oh, we can have wonderful house parties here, can't we, Willie?"

"We can, indeed. And, Daisy, you must redecorate every room to your own taste," Willie said.

"When I get all my own lovely things in here--it will be beautiful. I can see exactly how it will look."

They walked through the huge stables, examined with interest the kennels. "There is a load of space for dogs and horses," Daisy said happily.

"Hunting is the chief sport about here. There has to be a load of room for dogs and horses."

It took almost a year to redecorate Wellesbourne. But finally came the happy day when every piece of silver and crystal was in place, each painting hung, the fine carpeting down. The stables were filled with hunters and jumpers; the hounds and retrievers were at home in the kennels.

That evening Daisy walked again through all the rooms, enchanted. "I do want Mama and Papa to come over right away!" she cried. "And I want Mabel, too. Mabel must come. Oh, the parties and fun we will plan!"

At Wellesbourne--for the first time in her life--Daisy had all the pets she wanted. The dog population both in and out of the house gradually increased--it was almost impossible for her to resist buying a dog she fancied. Moreover, she had never forgotten Grandmother Kinzie's parrot. A parrot was added to the collection of pets. She had, too, the tame mocking bird she brought with her from Savannah. Guests at Wellesbourne soon became used to seeing Daisy move, always with dogs at her heels, a parrot on her shoulder, the bright little mocking bird following her about.

At Wellesbourne the Lows became more famous than ever for their hospitality. There mirthful crowds gathered for house parties, to ride to hounds, for pi-

95

geon shoots and grouse hunting. Each year when the Warwickshire Hunt Ball was held--and all the large houses in the country were filled with guests--an invitation to stay at Wellesbourne was highly prized.

Near Wellesbourne was the famous Warwick Castle, and the Earl of Warwick was a close friend of the Lows. A party at the Castle usually meant, too, a house party at the Lows', for Daisy and Willie always asked some of the celebrated guests to stay at Wellesbourne. The fabulous costume parties given by the Earl were among Daisy's favorite affairs. She always loved to dress up. She would spend weeks designing the costumes, fussing with handmade details. So eager was Willie to have everything correct that once when guests were to dress in the mode of Louis XV, he sent to Paris for a hairdresser who knew the proper way to dress the powdered wigs to be worn by the Lows and their guests.

Willie couldn't have brought anyone more popular to this English countryside than Daisy. She was an excellent horsewoman and loved to hunt--prime requisites in Warwickshire for popularity! But out of the field, into the drawing room, she was lovely to look at, witty and brilliant.

Even the Prince of Wales chided Willie for not having introduced Daisy to him more promptly after he waltzed with her at the Annual Yoemanry Dance.

It is possible that, at times, her English friends and neighbors were a little surprised by the projects Daisy undertook.

There was the matter of the blacksmith shop, for example.

Daisy had never been quite satisfied with the pair of gates that stood at the main entrance to Wellesbourne. She knew what they should be: iron gates, heavy and handsome, trimmed in copper. She sketched the design. And then decided to make them herself.

She went to the little blacksmith shop in the village, and talked the smith into taking her on as an apprentice. There in the stuffy, hot and smelly shop she worked day after day. When she discovered that in order to make the design she wanted, special tools had to be made, she fashioned the tools herself. Having learned the craft of iron-mongering, she moved a forge onto the estate at Wellesbourne and went to work.

"Daisy's anvil chorus!" friends and neighbors laughingly called it as the metallic hammering continued.

By the end of the winter, the gates were finished, and all admitted they were beautiful.

"But very expensive," Daisy commented, "the muscles of my right arm developed so I can't get my arm into any of my dresses!"

Though she was mistress of Wellesbourne, Daisy was still Daisy! When she heard of a poor old woman in the village who was sick and shunned by all because she was supposed to have leprosy, Daisy slipped away to see her, a basket of food on her arm. As the visits continued, Daisy was no longer able to keep them secret.

Willie worried, "Do you think you should go? They say she has leprosy. Do you think it is safe?"

"She hasn't leprosy!" Daisy scoffed. "She's sick and lonely and old. Besides," she looked at Willie shrewdly, "who are you to talk of safety? Planning to ride that wild horse of yours over the world's most dangerous course in the Grand National!"

Because they both enjoyed hunting and fishing, the Lows also bought a large lodge and hunting preserve in Scotland. This rough, rugged country Daisy grew to love.

Usually late summer and early fall found them at Lude, in Scotland. There, as at Wellesbourne, they were surrounded by guests. The Prince of Wales came for grouse shooting, the Earl of Warwick and other friends to stalk deer. The lodge was almost always full!

Through the years, too, Daisy and Willie did a great deal of traveling. There were, of course, frequent trips to the continent, to France, Switzerland, southern Italy and Spain. There were also trips back to the States, to see the family in Savannah, to visit old friends in the East.

But there were also exciting, long-remembered trips to the Orient, to Egypt, India and Africa.

Each place they visited, they found friends and made new friends. It was quite true that the Lows could go almost anywhere in the world and find themselves welcomed.

Nine

WAR IS DECLARED

On one of Mabel's visits with Daisy in England, she met a young friend of the Lows, Rowland Leigh. Much to Daisy's delight, they became engaged. Now she would have a sister in England.

"With both of us living here, Mabel, surely Mama and Papa will come over more often!" Daisy said happily. "And the rest of the family, too!"

Through the years, Daisy's bond with home continued to be very strong. Almost every letter home begged some member of the family to come to London for the season, to join her in Scotland in the Fall, to go with her on a trip to the Continent.

Her pride in her own country never diminished. And nothing pleased her more than to bring her British friends, as her guests, to her native land.

When Lord Herbert Vane-Tempest and the Earl of Warwick suggested a fishing trip, Daisy cried, "Oh, take them to Florida, Willie, for tarpon fishing. There's nothing like it any place else in the world! Tarpons weigh two hundred pounds or more--and sometimes you land one with a shark clinging to its tail! It's the most exciting sport." She added, "But we will go to Savannah first--you must see Savannah."

Sometimes Daisy and Willie opened their own home in Savannah for these visits. But if the stay was to be a short one, the guests always were graciously welcomed into the Gordon home.

Daisy would smile proudly as the visitors admitted that they had never tasted anything as delicious as the little oyster crabs browned in butter; that no food in Europe could compare with it.

After dinner she would take them to the beautiful old garden beside the house and say, "Now you will hear music such as you have never heard before." Then soft, true Southern voices would rise sweetly in old plantation songs and spirituals.

When the last song was sung, and the guests agreed they had never heard anything like the haunting melodies sung at dusk in the Southern garden, Daisy would promise, "Tomorrow morning Papa and I will show you something you've never seen before!"

In the bright morning they would drive out into the country a little way, until they reached a large shed. Inside the shed the guests saw nothing but a pool of water surrounded by straw. Papa whistled softly, and suddenly hundreds and hundreds of little black heads peeked out of the water.

"Terrapins! Now watch . . ." Within a few seconds the turtles were climbing onto the straw, pushing and crawling over each other, to get the food Papa put down.

As the guests exclaimed in surprise and delight, Daisy would say, "But just wait until you taste them in stew! You've never eaten anything so good! They even put oyster crabs in the shade!"

Watching her pride as she entertained her British guests, or hearing her urge, in England, friends to visit America, Willie Low would laugh and say, "Daisy, no matter how long you live in England and travel over the face of the globe, in your heart you'll always be an American and a Southerner."

In a measure this was true. One of their great jokes was the time, on a trip to Egypt, when the native band in the place they were dining played "Marching Through Georgia." The poor band leader thought the piece a compliment to anyone from Southern United States. He had no idea it was an insulting reminder of bitter defeat to a Southerner! Daisy--and Mabel, who was traveling with her--were very angry. As an apology they demanded the band play "Dixie." But the band did not know "Dixie." In fact, the Egyptian musicians had never heard of it. At Daisy's insistence, she and Mabel sang and whistled the tune until the band caught the air and were able to beat out something that could be recognized as "Dixie."

With her intense loyalty to her native land, when the first rumblings of the Spanish-American War reached England, Daisy planned to go to the States. If her country were to be involved in another war, she wanted to be of service.

As soon as war was declared, Daisy's father again answered the call to arms, although he was not a young man. He was put in charge of an infantry brigade stationed near Miami, Florida.

One of Papa's chief worries was that so many of his men became ill from drinking bad water. While attempts were made to check the water supplies and prevent pollution, the situation seemed impossible to control. More and more of the men fell ill. Soon hospital facilities were inadequate. In order to make room in the hospitals for the critical cases, sick men were being dismissed and sent back to service before they were physically fit for it.

When General Gordon wrote home and told his wife of this situation, she immediately packed up and went to Miami to start a convalescent hospital.

So, on Daisy's arrival in the United States, she found her work waiting for her. Mama needed help.

She particularly needed the kind of help Daisy would be able to give.

With characteristic energy and enthusiasm, Daisy flew into the work, doing as much as two other people might have done. Her wit and charm kept the men in good humor, and a dozen times a day Mama said, "I don't know how I could have managed without you."

One of the hospital's main problems was a shortage of food. Supplies in the vicinity were limited. Much of the food that came in was not fresh.

"Sick men can't get well without good, nourishing things to eat," Daisy said. "If the supplies don't come to us, I'll go to them."

So every morning she covered the countryside in a horse and buggy, searching the farms for food. Where she saw cows in a pasture, she drove straight up to the farmhouse and wheedled the farmer into selling her a share of the milk. When she sighted a flock of plump chickens, she was at the door, cash in hand, to bargain for poultry. Fresh fruit, eggs, vegetables, a smoked ham if she was lucky--all these she bought in whatever quantities she could, and carted them back to the hospital.

But as shortages continued and demands rose, it was sometimes difficult to find food even on the farms. There came a day when there was very little to take back to Mama, who was always waiting eagerly to see what Daisy had.

But Daisy's eyes were sharp. When she returned to the hospital, cases of canned goods were in the back of the buggy. "I can get more, too--but this was all I could carry this trip."

"What is it?" Mama asked.

"Don't let the men know. But it's really baby food. A good, nourishing formula based on milk."

The men ate the "pudding" gratefully, until the day one of them discovered the empty cans. When Daisy handed out the bowls of food that night, they refused to eat! The backbone of the American army eating pap that was meant for infants and nursing mothers? Take it away!

The following morning the men again refused the food. Daisy looked at their stubborn faces. They had to eat! She thought a moment, hesitated in indecision, then went to the kitchen.

There was a brief argument with one of the men helpers. Reluctantly he took a bottle from its hiding place, and Daisy poured a little of the liquid into a pitcher. Back to the ward she went. Into each bowl of "pap" went a few dark brown drops.

"Now it's no longer baby food," she said sternly. "It has rum in it. Eat it up."

The men laughed. Her ingenuity had defeated them. They ate the "pap."

"I suppose some people might criticize me for that," Daisy remarked to Mama; "but there are times when a person has to be practical. Sick men must eat."

The time spent at the hospital was hard. The weather was hot, the work exhausting. It was a far cry from the life Daisy had been leading abroad. But to this she never gave a thought. She had come home to be of service and was delighted to find a place where she was really needed. Also, opportunity to be close to the work with her mother, to have her father nearby, was a great joy.

When the war was over, she returned to England.

But Daisy did not return to a happy life when she went back to Wellesbourne. Willie was sick. Now she was to know several years of grief and unhappiness. She watched his condition grow steadily worse, his disposition, his mentality sicken and change as he became physically weaker.

Toward the end of his life his condition even necessitated their living apart. These were sad times for Daisy.

Willie Low died in 1905. They had been married nineteen years. While the last few years were very sad ones, Daisy had many years of happy memories with her husband--and these she always cherished.

Through the years after his death--as long as she lived--those close to Daisy would hear her say once in a while, "Something nice is going to happen today. . . . I dreamed of Willie last night."

Ten

FOREIGN LANDS

Papa said, "I think the very nicest thing about our Golden Wedding was that all our children were there." Mama smiled and nodded. The last guest had departed, and the family, everyone tired but triumphant, lingered briefly in the front drawing room to talk over the happy and exciting day.

"Mama, you looked beautiful," Daisy said.

"You, Daisy, quite outshone me."

"Oh, Mama, nobody could outshine you," Daisy exclaimed, then added contentedly, "but I did look grand, didn't I?"

"All my children did. I was very proud," Mama said. She touched the golden wreath in her hair. Fifty years earlier she had worn the same delicate wax flowers, only they were white then. "You did a lovely job of gilding the wreath, Daisy. The flowers look like pure gold! And the gift--it is so beautiful." Once more she walked over to the table and looked with happy eyes at the gold coffee service on the gold-edged crystal tray. "Aren't the little sugar tongs sweet?" She turned to the family, "Every piece is exquisite, and again, I thank you one and all."

A melody of chimes told them it was midnight, and past time to go. As Daisy rose, her brother Bill asked, "How long are you staying in Savannah, Daisy?"

"Just a few days. I must be in New York the first of the week. We are sailing on the *Majestic*."

"You'd better cancel your reservations and stay on for a while," Arthur suggested.

Eleanor laughed, "Don't say that! Daisy is taking Beth with her, and if she canceled I would have the most disappointed child in the country!"

"No, I won't cancel," Daisy said quickly, "I must go--but I'll be back before too long."

"Where are you going this time?" Mabel asked.

"First to Paris--then I don't know. Probably Ceylon--Calcutta. I'll give Beth some choice in the matter."

"Sounds like a wonderful trip," Arthur commented. "I'll wager you can almost lay claim to being the most traveled woman in the world. It seems to me you're always just back from some place, or just going."

"And always generously taking some of the young people with her," Mama added.

It was true. Especially in the years just following Willie's death, Daisy did a great deal of traveling. And, because she loved young people, on most of the trips she invited a niece or a nephew, or the child of a friend, to go with her.

A trip with Aunt Daisy was highly prized by the young set! Since she was entirely fearless and loved adventure, she was willing and eager to go any place, and words of caution were not in her vocabulary.

Those who had not been warned were a little startled the first night out if they shared a stateroom with Daisy. Startled and worried. For Daisy always insisted on having the upper berth, saying it was roomier, then proceeded to retire with a book, spectacles, writing portfolio and pen, an alcohol stove, a small kettle of water, tea caddy, teapot, tea-strainer, sugar and spoon.

She would explain, "I often sleep badly and like to brew myself a cup of tea during the night. Now go to sleep--I've never set fire to anything yet."

Those children who were too young to go with Daisy shared the trips too. Among the times she loved best on her visits home were those when she gathered the youngsters around her and told them stories.

She would sit on the floor, the children snuggled close, and tell them of the strange sights, the beauty and adventure that awaited them in foreign lands.

Then even the littlest ones would listen, quiet and fascinated, hours on end.

One of Daisy's favorite countries was India, and the children loved to listen to her stories of travel there. Some of her experiences were so familiar to them, the older ones would prompt her if she forgot a detail.

She would start with Ceylon. "It's a country of vivid color and brilliant sun," she would say, "trees, vines, bushes and shrubs, bright green and gigantic. And the people are as bright as the scene. Their bronze bodies--the laborers wear only loin cloths--are beautifully made and wonderfully graceful. Both the men and women have long hair, and the men, not the women, wear curious tortoise-shell combs in their hair. The women make up for the lack of ornamental combs with rings--rings in their noses, rings on their fingers and toes, and great quantities of bracelets strung on their arms. . . . In Ceylon you can walk right out and pick cloves, nutmegs, cinnamon and allspice in your own back yard. And all the hills are covered with tea! It's in Ceylon, too, you will see the flycatcher orchid. Horrid things--speckled with brown, and a mouth like a toad! But I daresay we could use a couple of them nicely on our front piazza!"

The children laughed. In the small silence that followed, young Arthur said, "In India children get married; don't they, Aunt Daisy?"

"Yes, indeed. It was in the holy city of Benares that your cousin Beth and I saw a seven-year-old bride in a wedding procession. The British prohibit their marrying younger than that. Personally, I think the bride exaggerated her age. But anyhow, there she was on her way to the temple to be married to a boy fourteen years old. We stopped the procession to see the bride. She wore a full watermelon-pink veil that completely swathed her, so that all you could see of her was the top of her head which was covered with silver ornaments, and her fingers and toes, which were laden with rings. When they lifted her veil so we could see her face, we were sorry we had stopped the procession. The poor little thing was pale and frightened, and kept her eyes tightly closed so she would not see us. Her bridegroom looked away when the veil was lifted. He was a handsome boy, with a sensitive, serious face, and I'm sure he resented our intrusion.

"When you go to India, if you go at the right time and to the city of Lucknow, you will see one of the most beautiful sights in the world. There the people gather together thousands and thousands of shells and tiny bowls. These they fill with oil, and put a small wick in each bowl. The bowls are set four inches apart along all the buildings and streets. At night they are lighted, and the whole city is twinkling with tiny golden lights. Really, it's too beautiful for words! Then the priests come out in their lovely lemon-colored robes, and hang garlands of marigolds around your neck. Only--the marigolds aren't there for long, because the little monkeys dart out of the trees to snatch them off you, and shamelessly eat them right in front of your eyes."

"There are always festivals in India, aren't there?" one of the older children urged Daisy on.

"Oh, yes; the people of India have all sorts of festivals! But my favorite one is the one the people of Benares hold once a year. Benares is on the Ganges--a swift and very blue river. One day a year it is the custom for all the people of Benares--men, women and children--to go down to the Ganges to bathe and wash their garments. All of them go into the water fully dressed, carrying clean clothes. The women wear seven yards of cloth, which they drape around themselves, and a turban. In some magic fashion, they are able to stand up to their chins in the river, and change their clothes while exposing nothing more than their heads, and occasionally a hand. Then the soiled clothes are washed, and the bathers walk out into the sunshine to let their garments dry--they dry very quickly. But imagine! A city of 390,000 people--all clean at one time!"

If the stories threatened to stop, one or another child was sure to say, "And tell us about the tiger." So

Daisy would tell of the fierce tiger that escaped from its cage and went berserk in the crowded bazaar, frightening all the people. "But the keeper remained calm," she related, "and said to the animal, 'Oh, tiger, please come home.' And the tiger did."

"What was the best of all about India?" the children would ask her.

"The birds and animals." The answer was always prompt and the same. "The beautiful parrots in the trees, the monkeys roaming everywhere, the little birds so tame they come right into your room and admire themselves in your looking glass."

So the children listened, enchanted, as she told of her travels in every part of the world. When she left them, there was an empty place no other adult could fill.

But no matter where Daisy went, Christmas usually found her back in Savannah.

Christmas was the time everyone came home who could. Then the big house was filled once more with children. Eleanor and her family, the Parkers, came down from New Jersey for the holidays. The youngest sister, Mabel, brought her two children over from London. The brothers, Bill and Arthur, lived nearby in Savannah with their families. But on Christmas, they must be packed in too.

"Christmas Eve I want everybody here," Mama would

say. "We'll find room for all." And they always did.

As the holiday approached, the children would begin to ask, "Is Aunt Daisy coming?" . . . And the grown folks would inquire of one another, "Have you heard anything from Daisy?"

Sometimes she did write or wire. But more than likely, just about the time they were ready to give her up, an overladen cab would stop in front of the house and there would be Daisy!

Her arrival was anything but quiet. There was always at least one yapping, snapping Pekingese under her arm, and sometimes two. There was always a noisy, scolding parrot in a cage--until bringing birds into the country was prohibited by law. With glad cries of greeting, Daisy would sweep into the house, followed by a driver carrying more luggage than he could manage, and still more bundles to be brought in. Then the house would echo with, "Daisy's here-- Aunt Daisy's come. . . ."

"Don't touch Stink-pot Hairy Boy," she would warn the children who approached the Peke she held, "he bites. Isn't he beautiful? And Eleanor, don't come too close to Polly Poons. Remember--the parrot can't bear women. Only me. She loves men."

Eventually things would quiet down. Daisy would sit in a chair, Pekingese in her lap, the gray parrot or her big fierce blue macaw on her shoulder, and say,

"Now tell me all about yourselves--every one!"

For Daisy, Christmas was as exciting as it was for the children. She loved giving presents, and she loved receiving them.

The gifts she gave she chose with greatest care and joy. Often she took time to make them herself-- a set of hand-painted dishes, a miniature of a favorite child, or an exquisitely modeled head. When it came to the young people she seemed always to know which child wanted a pony more than anything else in the world, which boy wanted a dog. A young niece would receive a beautifully carved necklace from the Orient, a jewel from an Egyptian tomb, or, perhaps, a length of cobwebby hand-made lace Daisy brought her from Brussels for a new party dress. Whatever the gift, it was different from the gifts most grownups gave, and certain to please.

But apart from the gifts, the day itself--always celebrated in the same way at the Gordon home--held a special enchantment for her. Christmas Eve with Papa gathering the whole family together in the library, holding the youngest child on his knee, and reading them "The Night Before Christmas." . . . The gifts, mysterious and tantalizing in their wrappers, piled high in Mama's room. . . . The shouts, almost before daylight, of "Merry Christmas, Merry Christmas to all," ringing through the big house. . . . Then the packages to open, everyone talking at once, "Oh, look . . . do you really like it? . . . how beautiful . . . let me see. . . ." And the children's happiness to be shared. . . . Dinner in the afternoon, the grownups around the large oval table, the children seated at a side table all their own. . . . And at night, the fireworks at the "Park Extension," which even the littlest child was allowed to stay up and watch, fireworks filling the sky with ribbons of light, bursts of color, clusters of falling stars. A brilliant end to an exciting day!

Although Daisy often made only a short visit at Christmas, and had traveled thousands of miles to reach Savannah, the day was always worth the trip.

Eleven

SEVEN GIRLS IN SCOTLAND

The gentleman seated next to Daisy at the luncheon table was most interesting. Daisy had heard of him before--who in England hadn't?--as the great defender of Mafeking in the South African War. Now she learned that as an officer in the British army he had been stationed in India. And India she loved. More than that, he was a descendant of Captain John Smith, a pioneer and adventurer whom Daisy greatly admired. Daisy and the fine-looking gentleman had lots to talk about.

So the following summer, when she was inviting guests to the castle she now took for the hunting season in Scotland, Sir Robert Baden-Powell was among them.

The day after his arrival in Scotland, Sir Robert sat out on the lawn and watched Daisy as she modeled the figure of a child. Conversation had been spasmodic, mostly about the figure she worked on, until Daisy asked, "What is this Boy Scout organization I'm told you are interested in?"

Sir Robert smiled. "Are you just being polite? Or do you really want to know? For, I assure you, when I start talking about the Boy Scouts, it is rather difficult to stop me."

"I really want to know," Daisy answered, turning from her work.

"Very well, then I will start from the beginning. But you need not stop modeling. I will talk while you work."

Then Sir Robert told Daisy how the idea of the Boy Scouts had come to him, years before, when he was in India. There young troops were sent to him straight from school, well-grounded in the three R's, their heads full of theory. But they lacked self-reliance, they had not been taught resourcefulness. If they were sent out on a scouting mission and became lost or ran out of supplies, their lives were endangered because they did not know how to take care of themselves. Thus, in order to strengthen his regiment and teach the young men to be self-sufficient individuals, he worked out a special training program in effective scouting.

This experience proved to Sir Robert Baden-Powell that boys readily took practical training for outdoor life. He learned, too, that through this training they developed character, physical fitness, and trustworthiness. They became keener observers and learned to assume responsibility.

When Sir Robert had time, he wrote down his ideas, and in 1908 the Boy Scouts were founded by him in England.

"So, you see," Sir Robert said, "the organization is only three years old. But almost every boy who hears of Scouting wants to join a troop. It is growing fast!"

"I should think it would!" Daisy exclaimed enthusiastically. "But why should it be limited to boys? Couldn't there be a similar organization for girls?"

Sir Robert's eyes twinkled. "Oh, the girls were keen for the idea right from the start. Although they had no organization, they began emulating their brothers, forming troops, copying the boys. At our first big rally in the Crystal Palace, a few sisters appeared, wearing khaki shirts and wide hats. And I can't begin to tell you how many letters I received from girls, demanding an organization of their own! Although we had not particularly encouraged girls to take up Scouting, by the fall of 1909 six thousand girls were doing so. I then realized afresh something I have always known: it is no good standing out against women, even very young ones, when they have once set their hearts on anything."

Sir Robert then told Daisy how, in November of that year, he offered "A Scheme for Girl Guides," in which he explained why the Girl Guides were needed, and made suggestions for starting training, leadership and organization. In it he also outlined Second and First Class tests and a list of proficiency badges.

He changed the name from "Scouts" to "Guides," and suggested blue uniforms instead of khaki. These changes he made partly to avoid resentment on the part of the Boy Scouts who might not want their sisters to copy their name and uniform. Partly, also, it was to avoid antagonizing parents, who might think Sir Robert was setting up an organization that would make tomboys of their daughters.

As request for help in forming new troops of the Guides came pouring in, Sir Robert, whose time was largely taken up with the Scouts, asked his sister, Agnes Baden-Powell, to take charge of the Guides.

This was a wise choice. For, as Sir Robert feared, many grown people disapproved of the Guides. They thought that girls wearing neckerchiefs and knickers, equipped with Scout knives and haversacks, were definitely "unladylike." They did not want their daughters rushing around the country, forgetting their manners.

However, Agnes Baden-Powell was a woman of great charm and gentility. Anyone meeting her knew at once that the organization would not foster unlady-like manners in the girls who joined it. Thus she did much personally toward breaking down existing prejudices.

As Sir Robert unfolded this story, Daisy stopped her work and listened intently.

When he finished, Daisy sat silent and thoughtful for a moment.

"Yours is a life of great usefulness," she said with admiration. "I feel that I am of so little use to anyone. It disturbs me greatly at times. . . ."

"I am sure many would deny that," Sir Robert answered. "Besides, it is difficult to say where our usefulness lies."

Daisy covered the unfinished figure with a damp cloth and put the modeling tools in their box. She stood looking out over the rough countryside for several minutes. Her thoughts turned to the girls who lived down there in the scattered farmhouses of Glen Lyon. Fair, clear-skinned Scottish girls who left home far too young, left for kitchens in London because there was nothing to do in the lonely Perthshire Valley. They and their families managed to eke a bare living from the swampy soil. But theirs were meager lives with very little social life and never a penny to spend.

Daisy turned suddenly to Sir Robert. "Why couldn't I start a Girl Guide troop right here in Glen Lyon?"

"No reason," Sir Robert answered. "As soon as I return to London I'll have my sister send you a copy of 'A Scheme for Girl Guides' to help you get started. . . ."

One morning, a short while later, Daisy sent for her housekeeper.

"Bella," she said, "we are having several girls for tea this afternoon--I don't know just how many. But I want plenty of cakes and tarts and scones and jam--everything girls like."

Bella's black eyes grew brighter, her pink cheeks pinker, and she stared at her mistress. Bella had run Daisy's households for many years now and was accustomed to sudden whims, to changes of mind. But from where was this crowd of girls coming? For once the house was empty of visitors--no guests were expected.

Daisy explained, "I'm starting a troop of Girl Guides, Bella, and I've invited every girl in Glen Lyon to come here to the first meeting. I remember when I was young I was frightfully disappointed to be invited to someone's home and not given something good to eat. As a matter of fact, I still am! So I want to serve tea when the meeting is over."

Seven girls came, walking as far as six miles each way.

Daisy told them what the Girl Guides were, what the Glen Lyon troop would do. She beamed with satisfaction as Bella served the tea. Bella was Scottish, and she knew how frugally the county people in that part of Scotland lived.

The tea table was laden with food! Bella had not forgotten the pitchers of thick cream for the bowls of berries, the pats of sweet butter for the hot scones. These were luxuries in a country where the soil was too poor to grow grain and sustain cattle.

The girls were shy at first. The great castle had been a landmark to them all their lives. None of the girls had ever dreamed of being entertained there. This never occurred to Daisy--she was so delighted to have them come, and having such a fine time herself. So she soon put them at ease and their shyness wore off.

When Daisy learned how far they had walked, she wondered if they would come back to another meeting.

But they did. At first Daisy thought perhaps they came just for the tea. How they did eat! But after several meetings, she knew they were having fun, were interested in the things they learned.

Daisy took them into her kitchen, and taught them to cook. Not fancy dishes, but good, nourishing food she knew they could afford. "Plain food can be delicious, if it's properly prepared," she would tell them.

She took them into the gardens for lessons in horticulture. "You can grow these, too," she would say, and then add, "I'll save seeds for all of you."

Daisy bought art material for the girls, and taught them to draw. She gave them lessons in sewing, always providing pretty materials to delight them.

But she did not teach them all their lessons. Anyone visiting Daisy was pressed into service. If a guest had a particular talent, some special knowledge, it must be passed to the girls. When several young Guardsmen came as her guests, she wheedled them into teaching the girls how to march and drill, how to signal to one another from the nearby hilltops. The meetings were rich in variety and interest.

Although the Glen Lyon troop was getting along famously, Daisy would say to herself, "It's not enough. It's true, they come here and have a good time, enjoy the tea Bella serves, and learn a little about things they have never known before. But I'm doing nothing to help them solve their greatest problem--their need for money. It is this need that sends them off to the cities when they are scarcely grown."

One day as she puzzled over this problem, it suddenly occurred to her that men came in great numbers to Perthshire for shooting in the fall. Then all the little hunting lodges through the country were filled with people. Why couldn't the girls raise poultry and have chickens and eggs to sell these visitors?

When this proposition was put up to the girls, they thought it a good one. At once lessons in chicken raising began.

Daisy's only objection to this scheme was that it was seasonal. There were only a few weeks when the visitors were there to buy. She must find them an additional occupation.

Though the country was too poor to provide grazing land for cattle, it did grow sheep. And sheep grew wool. When the sheared wool was sold, it rarely brought much of a price. But, Daisy shrewdly figured, if the wool were spun into fine, high-grade yarn. . . . She would teach the girls to spin!

First she had to learn to spin herself. With her natural aptitude for any kind of handiwork, her love of arts and crafts, this took her a very short time. And the girls learned quickly, too!

When fall came and it was time for Daisy to return to London, she was gratified to find that each of her girls had a nice little flock of chickens. In addition to this, the girls had become so good at spinning that, after nightfall, they saved oil and spun in the dark.

"But how shall we sell our yarn?" the girls asked.

"Don't worry about that. I'll find a market for it," Daisy promised.

The first thing she did on her return to London was to go to a shop that made and sold hand-woven articles. She showed them a sample of the wool her girls had spun. Immediately the shop agreed to buy all the yarn the girls sent.

Opening her home on Grosvenor Street, Daisy supposed the winter ahead would be similar to those in the past. As always, she would do quite a bit of entertaining. There would be reunions with old friends. She would fill the house again with young people. She wanted Mama and Papa to come over for a visit. If they would not come, she would go to Savannah for Christmas. She would certainly do some traveling-- the winter before she had gone to Egypt! Perhaps the Continent this year. . . .

But something was wrong! She frowned and tossed the half-written invitation into the basket. Her pet mocking bird flew from her shoulder, snatched the pen she had just put down and waited to be chided. The blue macaw screamed "Mama, Mama" from his perch, and flew over to the desk chattering when he wasn't answered. Silent in thought, Daisy wondered why the things she had looked forward to in winters past seemed unimportant now. What did she want? Her eyes fell on a little figure she had modeled the summer before--one of her Scottish Girl Guides sitting on a low stool, absorbed with her knitting. Could it be that the Glen Lyon troop had taken a deeper hold on her than she had realized?

Throughout the summer, she had felt useful. She was helping a group of people who needed help--not by giving them money or things, but by giving herself. That was what she missed now--the feeling of usefulness!

Well, girls elsewhere needed help. Just that morning she had driven through a poor section of London and thought of the misery that must lie there. What of the girls in London's slums? Surely they needed new interests, learning, a wholesome social life as much--perhaps more--than the girls in Pertshire.

At Girl Guide headquarters, they were happy to hear that Daisy wanted to take charge of a London troop. It was particularly difficult to get leaders to start new troops in the poor sections of the city.

Daisy's first chore was to search the dingy streets until she found a room large enough for troop meetings. The meeting place must be near the girls' homes. For most of them had neither time nor tram fare to go out of their own neighborhood.

Daisy finally found a basement room on Charlotte Street that fitted the need. Then she invited the girls of the community to come and hear about the Girl Guides.

Not until a painter--whom she had hired to help her fix up the room--told her did Daisy realize a gruesome murder had recently been committed just a few doors away! "The girls might be scared to come around here," he said. "Folks are shunnin' Charlotte Street."

Daisy certainly hoped not! At any rate, she was going to be prepared for a crowd. So the night of the first meeting she went to Charlotte Street, with a large hamper of food that Bella had packed, china and silver. In one corner of the room she had placed a table with an alcohol stove so they could make tea.

To Daisy's great satisfaction, the girls came, although several of the timid ones did admit it took courage.

At each meeting in the basement room the number increased. The girls worked at handcrafts with pride and eagerness. They played games with a zest that delighted Daisy. When she saw how much happiness Girl Guiding brought them, she decided to start a second troop in another tenement district.

A friend offered her the use of a room in Lambeth--a very poor section of London. Perhaps news of the good times in Charlotte Street spread to Lambeth. At the first meeting, twenty girls were present. This was more than even Daisy had optimistically hoped for. Fortunately, Bella had learned that London girls are just as fond of good things to eat as those in Scotland, and there were plenty of delicacies for all.

As the weeks went by, and her two London troops flourished, another idea began to take shape in Daisy's mind. Girl Guiding was well rooted in England. It had able leaders and was spreading fast. It would continue to grow there. She had seen the pleasure, the lessons in usefulness, it brought the girls in Scotland and to girls in London. It shouldn't be limited to young people of any one land. Now her dream was to take it to the girls of her own country.

Almost at once Daisy began to make preparations for returning to the States. Before leaving England, Daisy saw her two London troops put into the hands of good leaders. She left money to provide for the tea parties she and the girls had enjoyed at each meeting. She wrote the Scottish troop and was assured they were carrying on the work as well as they could without her. The London shop promised to continue buying their yarn.

On January 6, 1912, just three months after she had started the first troops in London, Daisy sailed for the United States. Sir Robert Baden-Powell was taking the same ship, starting on a round-the-world trip to visit Boy Scouts in other lands. Thus Daisy would have ample opportunity to discuss her plans with Sir Robert.

Sir Robert was enthusiastic about the idea of bringing Girl Guides to America. Daisy spent hours every day with him, asking questions, taking notes, making plans for the new project.

She was wise enough to know that a movement of

this kind needed proper promotion and the right start. She had a great deal to learn from Sir Robert and a short time in which to learn it. As he watched her, he marveled. She was no longer a young woman. She was partially deaf and physically rather frail. She knew the job ahead was a big one and a hard one. Yet she was throwing herself into it with the enthusiasm and energy of a girl!

As they walked the deck, talking over plans, or sat in the salon putting plans on paper, an attractive young lady named Miss Olave Soames often joined them. By the time the ship docked at Jamaica where Daisy was to leave by another ship for Savannah, Sir Robert and Miss Soames were engaged to be married.

And Daisy--with Sir Robert's promise of further advice and encouragement--was burning with eagerness to put her plan in motion, to start Girl Guiding in her own native land.

*T*welve

"FOR THE GIRLS OF AMERICA"

When Daisy announced her plan to her family, opinions differed.

"But Daisy's so impractical," was one comment.

"She isn't really impractical," Mama remarked; "she just does things differently from most people."

"That's true," Papa said. "You probably remember the time she invited a large crowd of guests for terrapin stew, only to discover after they had all arrived that the terrapin was spoiled? Daisy sent a servant out for more terrapin, then quietly lay down on the sofa and napped--or pretended to--while the guests played whist around her. When the cook announced the stew was ready to be served, she was once more the charming hostess. Most women would have fussed and apologized--but not Daisy. I thought it a very sensible way to behave."

"Won't her deafness be a handicap?" they asked.

"Daisy's deafness is unfortunate, of course," Mama said. "But I doubt that it's ever been a handicap to her in accomplishing an end. In fact, all of us know times when she's turned it to her advantage." Mama chuckled. "You've all traveled with her--you know that when the baggage man tells her her trunk can't be delivered in less than twenty-four hours, she smiles charmingly and says, 'Oh, thank you very much. That's very kind of you. I'll wait right here while you get it.' And she does, too. No, I doubt if her deafness will hinder her work. At any rate, she will never hear the word 'No' even when it is shouted very loudly."

Eleanor said thoughtfully, "She's so free to do as she wishes--won't Daisy mind being tied down to a project of this sort?"

Papa spoke quickly, "While Daisy's life for some years was carefree--you know that it was never frivolous. She has never taken things lightly. And make no mistake, whenever and wherever she was needed, Daisy was always there. Even if it meant personal inconvenience, even discomfort."

"Well, whatever the hazards and tribulations ahead are, you may be sure nobody can talk Daisy out of her plans now," Arthur, Daisy's youngest brother, said. "She says the organization can be planted here in the States and that she will prove it. She won't back out, you may be sure."

Mama laughed. "Do you remember, Eleanor, the first time Daisy 'proved' something? She had been told her hair was taffy color--it was when she was little--and that delighted her. Then Bill, teasing, said it wasn't taffy color at all, but just plain light brown. A few days later you children had a taffy pull, and Daisy made Alice braid strips of taffy into her hair. Sure enough, her hair and the taffy were exactly the same color."

"And if I remember," Eleanor finished the story, "the taffy hardened and you couldn't get it out. You had to whack her hair off and she looked a sight for weeks."

"Yes," Mama agreed, "that is true. But she did prove it. Arthur is right. Nobody can talk her out of it now. And I don't think anyone should try. Daisy has always loved young people. You know how much affection she has lavished on all the younger ones in our family--first on her younger brother and sisters, then on all the nieces and nephews, their friends, and the children of her own friends."

"And it hasn't been just a matter of Daisy's giving them gifts and parties and trips abroad," Bill pointed out. "She's always been willing to do things for youngsters most grownups don't want to be bothered doing."

"She has indeed," Eleanor added. "For example--

her willingness always to spend hours at the bedside of a sick child, telling stories and making up games, and acting as if it were the nicest way on earth to spend a day. . . ."

"Yes, Bill and Eleanor are right," Mama said. "Daisy's always been willing to give a great deal of herself to make young people happy. I think it is a splendid idea for her to start this work with girls."

"I think so too," Papa agreed. "And we must not discourage her."

On reaching Savannah, Daisy had wasted no time getting her plan under way.

First she phoned several of her friends: "I have something for the girls of Savannah, and all America—and all the world! You must come right on over," she said. "We're going to start it tonight."

A few days later she invited the girls who attended a nearby school for tea.

She showed them pictures of the English Girl Guides, and told them about the organization as she had seen it working. The Savannah girls were enthusiastic. They wanted a troop, too.

So many girls responded to Daisy Low's invitation that two troops were formed on that March afternoon. As she wrote down the names of the first troop, her own niece and namesake, Daisy Gordon, headed the list.

The carriage house behind her home would serve

as troop headquarters. When the girls wanted to play outdoor games, they could use a vacant lot she owned across the street.

Now Daisy talked "Girl Guides" to everybody in Savannah! Many people were frankly disinterested. Some were opposed to the organization. The girls of Savannah had done very well so far without any such nonsense and they saw no reason for putting new notions into their heads. Others simply smiled patiently at Daisy's enthusiasm and thought, "If she wants to play around with this idea, there is no harm in it."

But there were those who saw, as she did, the need for the organization and could visualize its growth, its value to girls all over the nation in the years to come. These few rallied to her aid.

There were six troops active in Savannah when Daisy decided she had to return to England. For one thing, she wanted to study more thoroughly the Girl Guides. She wanted to spend time at the English headquarters and learn how the organization functioned, how their leaders were trained for the work.

When she left, all she could give the Savannah leaders was the English Girl Guide handbook and pictures of the uniforms for the American girls to copy. She promised to return in the fall.

While Daisy was in England, the Savannah troops worked hard. One of their more difficult chores was making their own uniforms. They tried to copy the uniforms worn by the English Girl Guides from the pictures Daisy had left. They did not even know what kind of cloth to make them of, nor what color to choose.

Finally a dark blue duck was decided on, with light blue sateen ties. Now came the work of cutting and pinning, sewing, ripping and recutting until they finally evolved uniforms that closely resembled those in the pictures.

In planning meetings and working out requirements, they followed the English handbook as nearly as they could. They took hikes and kept bird notebooks. Substituting American sports for English ones, they formed basketball teams and played intertroop games. They would have a great deal to report when Daisy returned.

Ordinarily, Daisy would have stayed on in Scotland through the fall. But now she had two reasons for returning to the States early in September. She wanted to get back to her Guides. And she wanted to spend the month of September with her father and mother. On her previous visit to Savannah she was so completely wrapped up in getting the Guides started, she had spent a minimum amount of time visiting with the family.

But instead of the happy months she planned with

her parents, a great sorrow awaited Daisy. On September 12th her father died after a brief illness. Daisy had loved him very deeply. His death was a tremendous shock.

Work, for her, was the best medicine. She threw herself into Girl Guiding heart and soul. Back in Savannah, she listened eagerly to the story of the troops' progress.

"Did anything go wrong?" she asked anxiously. "Anything that might give people a wrong impression about Guiding?" She well knew how important it was in these early days not to have anything happen that might prejudice people against the movement.

One of the leaders laughed. "At an early meeting, the girls became a bit too enthusiastic over the lessons in first aid," she reported. "After the meeting they went, as they always do, to Solomon's Drug Store for sodas. Having just completed a lesson in bandaging, they decided to buy adhesive and gauze, and put to practical application their recent knowledge."

"A good idea," Daisy interrupted.

"Yes, except that, having bandaged each other up, they went by the home of one of the girls, where most of their mothers were attending a card party. When the mothers saw their daughters come in, with heads and legs bandaged, arms in slings, several women fainted! There was quite a little excitement until the girls explained."

Daisy laughed. "Well, it shows that they did a professional job of bandaging anyhow."

With great interest Daisy now watched the activities of her first troops of American Girl Guides.

She attended the meetings--which started always with the recitation of the Promise and the Laws, went into a discussion of the badges the girls were working toward and reports on what had been done toward those ends.

She went across the street to the corner lot and watched their games--the girls in wide, pleated gym bloomers, protected from the stares of passing people by canvas curtains hung on wires surrounding the playing field.

She saw that they had their first experience at camping out--five whole days of sleeping under the stars, cooking over open fires, fighting mosquitoes and avoiding poison ivy.

While she worked with these girls, watching them, the need for establishing a national organization of Girl Guides become more and more urgent in her mind. She discussed the idea with the Guide leaders in Savannah. She talked it over with her mother. Everyone thought the idea was a good one and a feasible one.

But Mama, knowing that launching a national organization was a vast undertaking, said to her, "It will mean giving up a great deal on your part, Daisy--your time will no longer be your own. You will have to go where you are needed, not, perhaps, where you wish to be. It will be physically and nervously exhausting. Before you start, be sure you are willing to make these sacrifices."

"Oh, Mama. I don't consider them sacrifices. More than anything in the world I want to give Guiding to girls--to all girls. Wherever I am needed, that is where I want to be."

Mama smiled and nodded. "Then go ahead."

Daisy wisely knew that if a national organization were to be successfully established, she would have to have the aid of many people in many parts of the country. So her first step was to write letters--letters to prominent people, to friends and acquaintances, in Boston, New York, Washington, Cincinnati, St. Louis, San Francisco--every place she knew someone who might help.

The replies she received were encouraging enough so that, in April, Daisy went to Washington to enlist the interest and aid of prominent women there. Washington, it was fairly well decided, should become the National Headquarters.

When Daisy left for Washington she took her mother with her. Mama now was in her seventies. But in spite of her age and the sorrow she had recently been through, Mama was as witty, as full of energy as ever, and with a zest for living that many a younger person envied.

In Washington Daisy was able to arrange for a committee of prominent women to meet at the White House.

During the past months, in addition to all her other work, Daisy had found time to rewrite the English Girl Guides' handbook, keying it to American girls. When she went to the White House, she proudly had under her arm printer's proofs of a new handbook called, "How Girls Can Help Their Country."

The women in Washington were quite enthusiastic about the idea of an American Scout organization for girls. Daisy was particularly pleased to find Mrs. Woodrow Wilson interested in the plan, for it was Daisy's wish to have the President's wife chief of the organization just as the President was of the National Boy Scouts.

All in all, "the Girl Scout Stampede at the White House," as Mama called it, was a success.

Daisy knew that the movement would not gain momentum unless she had prominent names behind it. Names that would give it prestige. This was needed first of all because it was new. And second because the very idea of Scouting for girls was startling and a little shocking to some people, just as it had been in

England. If it was to build force, it must receive the blessing and approval of well-known people.

So her next step was to go to most of the large cities and see people who would be helpful to her.

And now another problem had become large enough so that solving it was to take much of Daisy's time. As soon as her Girl Guides were fairly well established, Daisy began to hear from other women who had brought the idea of Guiding over from England, and started local troops in their own home cities. Most of these had taken the name Scouts, however, after the Boy Scouts, rather than retaining the English name Guides.

These troops posed a delicate problem. It was natural for each of the leaders to feel that she was an American founder, and to want recognition for her troop. The importance and value of these troops were fully recognized by Daisy. But she did not want to see them continue as independent, rival groups. She wanted them all to come in together as part of the national organization. With her usual graciousness and diplomacy, Daisy was able to bring these troops into the national organization successfully and amicably. And because they had called themselves Scouts, it was finally decided to give the organization the name Girl Scouts rather than Guides. In a way, this change of name was a disappointment to Daisy. But she felt that the most important and pressing thing was to get the organization strongly amalgamated and on a sound working basis. Arguing over the name was a waste of time--the girls would be served just as adequately if called Scouts as they were when called Guides.

Now her time was completely given over to meeting people, talking before groups, rushing to make trains, writing letters, hurrying on to still another appointment. Often she spent six or seven nights in a row, each night in a different place.

Wherever she went she assured people, "I want no money for the organization. I will finance it myself. All I want is your support."

In each city and town she tried, whenever possible, to meet with groups of girls and tell them of Girl Scouting. "We must always remember the organization is for the girls," she would say to those working with her. "We can have every prominent name in the country behind us, but it doesn't mean a thing if we don't give the girls what they want."

As Mama had said, Daisy's deafness was an asset in some ways. Unfortunately it had, through the years, grown worse as the good ear became affected. The continual strain to hear, the additional effort she had to make to cope with the physical handicap was undoubtedly a drain on her both physically and nervously. But Daisy did turn that handicap to her own uses.

When she asked someone to serve on a committee or to head a new troop, the most emphatic "No!" was met with her charming smile and "How good of you. I knew you would say 'yes.' What's that? Never mind. . . . Here is what you are to do. . . ."

In the spring of 1913, much to her dismay, Daisy found it necessary to return to England. There were problems regarding property to be rented and business affairs that demanded her attention. Since she was financing, alone, the entire Girl Scout organization she could little afford to neglect financial matters.

But there were so many things here to do!

Before leaving she had to get the final copy of the handbook to the publisher and exact a promise from him to put it in print as fast as possible. As more and more troops were organized it became increasingly important to put into the hands of leaders a book as a guide.

Then there was the matter of uniforms. It had become completely impractical for the fast-growing organization to use home-made uniforms. Uniforms had to manufactured. But Daisy did not want them to be so expensive that the girls would find their purchase a hardship. So there were days of hurrying from one manufacturer to another, climbing stairs to loft sewing rooms, examining materials, arguing over prices. Daisy finally found a manufacturer in Red

Bank, New Jersey, whom she considered satisfactory, and an order for uniforms was placed.

Early in the summer, having made her mother and her sister Eleanor promise to help carry on her Girl Scout work during her absence, she sailed for England.

As she feared, it took time to get matters settled in England, and the weeks stretched out. Her impatience grew when she heard nothing from the publisher and the news of her Scouts that reached her seemed very scanty!

Her one consolation was that several prominent Americans--whose support in Washington would be important to the organization--were visiting London. She seized this opportunity to entertain them and interest them in the Girl Scouts.

She visited the troops she had started in Lambeth and Charlotte Streets, and was happy to learn that they--as well as the troop in Scotland--were flourishing. But as the summer lengthened she became more and more eager to get back to her work in the States.

Optimistically she tried to assure herself, "If I were in the States, everybody I need to see probably would be away--in the mountains or at the seashore--through the hot weather. But if only I would hear about the handbook. . . ."

Finally, in September, she was able to clear up all

necessary business and sail for America. On her return she found that most of her worry and impatience were ill-founded.

Copies of "How Girls Can Help Their Country" were beginning to pour off the press. The little office she had rented in the Munsey Building, in Washington, was even busier than she had anticipated. Girls from all over the country were writing in wanting to start troops, asking how to organize, what to do.

Shortly after her return, the first of the new uniforms arrived.

Daisy lifted them out of the box. "Aren't they trim and nice?" She was pleased. "I do hope the boys won't howl about the color!"

At the request of the girls, the blue uniform had been discarded in favor of khaki. "If they do howl, we can't help it--the girls must have what they want. And," she added, "the blue wasn't nearly as practical, for it does show dust."

The boys did howl. Why should the girls copy their color? Daisy appeased them by announcing that blue uniforms would be manufactured for the girls in addition to the khaki ones, and they could take their choice.

Since all the girls chose khaki, and the blues went a-begging, the boys lost the argument. But they soon grew used to seeing Girl Scouts in khaki, and the matter was forgotten.

There were plenty of problems, each to be solved by ingenuity, tact, or just plain hard work!

While Daisy was in England, Sir Robert Baden-Powell, to whom she turned for help and advice, had said to her, "Given a year, a movement that has good in it will live."

Consequently the success of the Girl Scouts during its first year as a national organization was of great importance to her. She watched, gratified, as troops were started in various cities--troops in New Bedford, Massachusetts, in Washington, D.C., troops in and about Boston.

Recognizing the importance of interesting other leaders in the Girl Scouts, Daisy went to Baltimore to see Cardinal Gibbons and got permission to start troops in the Roman Catholic Settlement House there. She went to Chicago to visit Jane Addams at Hull House, where she lectured before groups of service leaders and aroused great interest in Girl Scouting. Wherever she spoke a spark of interest was fired, and Daisy lost no time in fanning it into a bright and steady flame.

Now people began to come to Daisy for help. The leader of a girls' club in Cincinnati, realizing her group needed better organization and a different program, went to New York to consult Daisy. Thus Girl Scouting was started in Cincinnati. And so it spread, faster and wider than Daisy had ever dared hope. At the end of the first year, she knew, as Sir Robert had said, the movement had good in it and it would live.

As it grew, Daisy was more and more alarmed to see how much it cost to finance. She had never been good at keeping accounts, even when she was a child in school. And her arithmetic, like spelling, did not improve with age.

"I'll just have to be less extravagent," she said sternly to herself one day. "Every penny I don't spend on myself is a penny saved for the Scouts."

That noon she pinned her new hat on her head, glanced at herself in the mirror with self-satisfaction, and went to have lunch with a friend.

During the course of the meal, she noticed her friend staring at the new hat.

In distress she cried, "What's wrong with my hat? The vegetables aren't wilting, are they?"

The friend laughed. "Indeed they are! I know vegetable ornaments on hats are stylish this year, but--"

"Oh, dear," Daisy sighed. "This very morning I decided I must be more economical and save my money for the Girl Scouts. Instead of paying to have my hat trimmed, I just went to the kitchen and picked up a beautiful perky carrot and some lovely parsley--I had no idea vegetables wilted so fast!"

"Oh, Daisy, the little you can save in small economies will never be enough!"

"Maybe not," Daisy said firmly, "but it will help. And I mean to keep on trying, even though my first attempt was not very successful."

$\mathcal{T}$hirteen

THE GREATEST VISION OF ALL

With much property in England, and many interests there, it was necessary for Daisy to make frequent trips abroad.

August, 1914, found her at Castle Menzies, in Scotland, facing--she knew it--the third war she was to live through.

For several days now the rumors spread like panic: "No trains will be allowed to run except for military purposes" . . . "Ports will be closed" . . . "London will be bombed. . . ."

Daisy set aside the miniature she was painting. She was worried. Would she be able to get Mama back to America--back where there would be plenty of food, no privations? Back where the war, perhaps, would never reach?

She looked at Mama, calmly knitting, apparently not the least upset. Mama had never been afraid of anything, war included!

"I'm worried about Mabel and her family in London," Daisy said. "I'm going to tell her she must come to us. After all, it's comparatively safe here. This glen leads to no place of importance. I have a supply of oil so we can use the oil stove, if, as they say, we won't be able to get coal."

Mama finished the row before she answered. "You may ask Mabel to come if you wish. I doubt if she will, though--any more than you will stay here if war is declared."

Bella came in from marketing to announce, "Food prices have doubled since yesterday, Mrs. Low."

"I'm not surprised, Bella. Everyone is frightened and laying in stores."

"Another thing, Mrs. Low. Cook is frightfully upset. She has a crippled niece, only three years old, in the Home at Dover. The Home has now been evacuated by order of the government, and the child--who is strapped to a board--has no place to go."

"Oh, Bella, how dreadful. But tell Cook not to worry--we will bring her here. We'll get her here--even if she has to be sent by parcel post!"

"Cook will be much relieved," Bella said, then asked: "But do you think we are certain to have war? Some in the village say not."

"I'm afraid war is inevitable," Daisy answered.

It came swiftly. Fortunately, Daisy was able to get Mama passage on an American ship that was guaranteed safe conduct to its own shores. But she gave up trying to talk Mabel into coming to Scotland. And, as soon as she saw the crippled child brought safely from Dover, her care arranged for, Daisy left for London.

She was torn now between the desire to rush back to the States to be with the Scouts, and the knowledge that she could be of great help if she stayed in England where everything was crippled by the suddenness of the war.

"There is so much to do here," she finally decided, "I'll keep in close touch with the Girl Scouts and go across the minute they need me."

In London the Girl Guides were organizing for war activities. There was a rush of work!

As the German army overran Belgium and pushed southwestward into France, refugees came pouring into England. Penniless, without shelter, often friendless, these war-torn people were desperately in need of help. When committees were organized to come to their aid, Daisy found herself also busy with refugee work.

Soon her home on Grosvenor Street was filled with refugees, and when there was no more room there she sent them to Castle Menzies.

In spite of the load of work she carried in London, she did not neglect the Girl Scouts. In what pieces of time she could snatch, she was rewriting the hand-book. She also kept a steady stream of letters going across the sea--telling the girls what the Guides were doing in war work, advising and counseling, asking questions. And a steady stream of letters came back to her--telling her of the new troops being organized, what the girls were doing, how the organization was growing.

When they wrote that all 5,000 copies of the handbook had been distributed, she decided she must get back to the States and see that the revised edition she had been working on was put into print.

"But it's so dangerous," her friends tried to discourage her. "The Atlantic is full of German submarines."

"Well, I certainly don't intend to let a few German submarines hamper me," Daisy answered. "I shall go back and forth as I find it necessary."

Indeed, there was another problem now that worried her a great deal more than submarines! It was a financial one. Not only had the cost of financing the Girl Scouts continued to increase, but some of her income was tied up due to the war. It was difficult--sometimes impossible--to collect rents. In addition, her great generosity kept her living costs very high.

She had to have money for the Girl Scouts. Where could she get it?

Daisy solved the problem by selling her pearls.

"The money from the pearls won't last forever," she said, "but it will make it possible to finance the organization for some little time at least."

To the distress of many, Daisy continued to cross the Atlantic whenever the need to be one place or the other was urgent. Not even the sinking of the *Lusitania* deterred her from making plans to return, in a few weeks, to England. In fact, the sinking made her angry, not afraid. "As neutrals, we Americans have a right to go where we please."

After the sinking, however, Daisy saw no possibility of the United States not being drawn into the war. In sorrow and anger she said, "By declaring war, we will hasten peace for the world. . . ."

Once again Daisy stood at a window and watched columns of men marching down a street. This time they were in khaki, and the street was Fifth Avenue, in New York. Daisy stood there, a slim figure in black. She was wearing mourning because, just a short time before, Mama had died. She watched with a heart full of sorrow--not only for her own loss, but for each of these men--the endless columns of men, on their way to fight a war on foreign soil.

But Daisy had little time for her own thoughts. Girl Scouts all over the country were now very active in war work. In the new and large National Headquarters in New York, things were humming. Daisy looked proudly at the first issue of the new magazine for Girl Scouts, *The Rally*. In that issue was the statement that membership in the organization was now 12, 812. At the Third Annual Convention, just closed, more than fifty delegates had come from all over the United States. In less than six years the Girl Scouts had grown from a group consisting of a handful of girls and a few personal friends to a large and expanding national organization.

Daisy turned back to the work that had been interrupted by the sound of the band and the marching feet. Packing cases and more packing cases to be labeled for shipment to troops in France. The cases were filled with Christmas gifts for men overseas-- thousands of packages that had come pouring in from Scout troops, gifts made by the girls, wrapped by them, now on their way to decorate Christmas trees in hospital wards and soldiers' barracks.

Before the Christmas packages had come in, the rooms were full of warm garments knitted by the Scouts, boxes of puzzles and scrapbooks they had made for the wounded, trench candles to light the dark dugouts.

Daisy was proud of the war work the girls were doing.

Many of the tasks they had chosen were not easy ones.

During the summer she had seen them at work on farms, raising vegetables, canning and drying the food for winter use.

In Washington, D.C., she had seen details of girls making as many as five hundred sandwiches a day for troops coming through, making them of jams they themselves had put up.

In the Red Cross workrooms she had seen the Scouts doing the hardest kind of work, with no expectation of recognition or reward--sweeping and cleaning rooms, staying on duty for messenger service in all kinds of weather, taking care of stock and supply rooms.

In Savannah she saw the young girls, including her niece and namesake, Daisy Gordon, working long hours every day, driving a car for the Motor Corps. Every place she went she saw girls busy with the grim task of helping wage a war on the home front.

While Daisy knew it was necessary, and was very proud of the work the girls were doing, she always regretted the fun they were missing.

To young Daisy's mother she said, "If they had tasted of the light-hearted life you and I and all of us used to lead, I would be more resigned to the hard service they are giving. How I wish they could have had their fun first!"

"Perhaps the work does develop character--and

independence," young Daisy's mother sighed.

"Even if it does, I feel rebellious for them. Oh, I wish the war was over, and I could gather up all the young people I know and take them to Florida tarpon fishing; wouldn't that be fun!"

The Liberty Loan Drive started, and the Scouts were busier than ever. Now in addition to the other work there were bonds to sell. And excellent saleswomen the Girl Scouts were, too! It was a proud moment for Daisy, and all the other Scouts, when word came from the Treasury Department that the girls had done so well, a beautiful medal, designed by Paul Manship, was to be struck and conferred on each Girl Scout who sold ten or more bonds to ten different people.

When peace came, the record of war work done by the Girl Scouts was a very fine one. What the girls did not realize was that, while they were helping their country, they were also helping the organization. Their war work attracted a great deal of favorable attention. A number of very fine and able women now turned to the Girl Scouts and offered their services.

In the meantime, the organization had grown to such proportions that it was impossible for Daisy to continue financing it alone. She was willing to sell all her jewels to meet expenses, but that was not the answer. At best, it could only postpone briefly the time when outside help must be asked for. Officers in the Girl Scouts had recognized this shortly before the United States went to war and had started then to try and raise some money to help meet expenses. As the value of the organization was more and more realized, people were enlisted to help financially. Daisy now was sometimes paid for the lectures she gave--not much, but something--and this went into the treasury.

The fact that people were contributing was a great relief to Daisy. The financial burden had been a very heavy one.

As soon as the Armistice was signed, Daisy boarded a ship and sailed for England. She wanted to give Sir Robert Baden-Powell a complete report on the growth of the Scouts and learn, too, what had been happening to the Guides since spring 1917, when America's entrance into the war made trans-Atlantic travel impossible.

In England, Daisy found that Lady Baden-Powell, who had been given the title "Chief Guide for all of Great Britain," had a new idea for Girl Guiding and Scouting.

Daisy listened with intense interest as the plan unfolded. When Lady Baden-Powell finished, Daisy exclaimed, "I think it is the most exciting plan I've heard since the day Lord Baden-Powell first told me of the Scouts!"

The plan was for the formation of an International organization for the Girl Guides and Girl Scouts. By now troops existed in many countries. But so far nothing had been done to integrate or bring together Scouts and Guides from different lands. The formation of an International Council would bring these national groups into one great, world-wide organization.

Daisy had always seen Scouting not as something for just the girls in Savannah, or even the girls of America, but for the girls of all the world.

"Your vision has always been so broad," Lady Baden-Powell said, "I thought you would find the plan interesting."

"Interesting! It is exciting! I want to help in every way I can."

All in all, that winter in London was a busy and happy one for Daisy. Scarcely a week passed that she did not make a trip to some English town to lecture in the interests of Girl Guiding and Scouting. In the city a great deal of time was taken up with meetings for the development of the International Council.

There were still a large number of American soldiers in England. As always, too, the house on Grosvenor Street was filled with guests.

Daisy wrote her friends in America, "Tell everyone you know who has a son over here to write him to come to my house."

And the boys came!

Bella was a little appalled at the first of these gatherings, when the rugs came up, the furniture was pushed to the walls, and the thump of soldiers' boots fairly shook the house. And the singing! She wondered that the neighbors didn't complain. The young people would gather around Daisy at the piano and, in their enthusiasm, each seemed to be trying to outsing the others. But none sang more enthusiastically than Daisy.

"Aunt Daisy, you're singing off key," a visiting niece criticized her.

If Daisy heard, she ignored this criticism, "I do sing nice and loud; don't I?" she answered happily.

For these gatherings, too, there was a never-ending supply of food. Once Bella thought Girl Guides could eat more than any other people on earth. Now she knew that tribute went to young American soldiers.

A few months after Daisy landed in England--on February 21, 1919--the International Council met, for the first time, at Guide Headquarters in London. Daisy was elected corresponding member for the United States. She was delighted--though she knew this would mean still more work and responsibility.

Now she talked "International Council" to all her friends. And when spring came, she made plans to return to her own land with the new program.

"It's been a most satisfactory winter," she said to her old friend, Rudyard Kipling, as they sat at tea in her drawing room. "But I'm eager to return to the States."

"When you go back, what are you going to do with Polly Poons, now that it's against the law to take parrots into the United States?" Kipling looked at the parrot who stared back at Kipling with a wicked eye.

"Why? Do you want to keep her?"

"Heavens, no! I was being curious--not helpful."

"Never mind. I have friends in Belgium who are taking her while I'm gone."

Kipling shook his head sadly, "Poor Belgium. Now her devastation will be complete! What the Germans have left of the country will be demolished by Polly Poons!"

Daisy handed the parrot a biscuit. "She's really beautiful. She sleeps on my chest."

Kipling shuddered. "There must be special good angels that look after and protect you. After riding in a car with you at the wheel, I suspected it. Now I'm conviced of it!"

"Nonsense! Never had an accident."

"Daisy, you are the only person in the world who can drive at a furious speed with one wheel over a precipice!"

They laughed. And as Kipling rose to go Daisy said, "For that, I won't offer to drive you to the station."

"When are you leaving for the States?"

"In May. And I'm hoping to persuade the Baden-Powells to go with me. I want them to see the magnificent work the Scouts are doing in America."

Lord and Lady Baden-Powell did accompany Daisy back to the States. Proudly she took them to National Headquarters to meet the leaders who were helping carry on the work. She took them to Pine Tree Camp--at Long Pond, on Cape Cod, where the first National Training School had just been moved. Wherever they went, advice was sought by both the Baden-Powells and the American leader. Methods were compared, opinions asked.

Perhaps this visit served to bring into sharper focus the necessary differences between American Girl Scouting and English Girl Guiding. At any rate, at about this time Daisy became keenly aware of the fact that the organization of the Girl Scouts had to be different from the Guides. In England, where the country was geographically small, a few, well-chosen leaders could easily keep the organization integrated and working with little machinery. But in a country as large as the United States, with an organization growing by leaps and bounds, this became complicated. Matters had to be worked out with groups of people--sometimes large groups.

Now Daisy began to wonder if the reins shouldn't be handed over to others.

She said, "I'm an autocrat--I know I am. I'm so sure my way is right, until some other way is demonstrated. I think it would be better, since we have a good solid national organization, if others took charge."

"But the Girl Scouts depend on you . . ."

"And I want the Scouts to feel always that they can depend on me," Daisy smiled.

"But you're the founder."

"I'll always be the founder."

"You should have some official title . . ."

"I want only to be known as Founder of the Girl Scouts of America--that is a proud title! I will continue to work for and with the Girl Scouts--but I believe the organization now needs new leadership."

It was not easy for Daisy to bow out as head of her beloved Girl Scouts. Only the fact that she wanted, always, the right thing, the best, for the organization made it possible for her to hand over the top place to others.

Resigning as Leader did not mean that work and responsibility for Daisy lessened. Rather the opposite. For, while she was not required to spend as much time and energy with the American Girl Scouts as she had before, she threw herself, with characteristic eagerness and enthusiasm, into the International side of Girl Scouting and Guiding.

This she now saw as the greatest vision of all. Through her beloved Girl Scouts and Guides, nations of the whole world would be linked in friendship and goodwill.

"It's going to mean a great deal of exhausting work, Daisy--travel, meeting people . . ."

Daisy brushed this aside. "Isn't it a glorious idea? Oh, I have so many plans for it! But I won't neglect my American Scouts. Indeed I won't!"

Fourteen
CAMPFIRE STORIES

"But, surely, Mrs. Low--you're not going out on a night like this!"

"I certainly am," Daisy said, stomping into her overshoes.

"Do you think the girls can get there?"

"I hope so. At any rate, I promised to be there, and I don't want to risk disappointing them. I can't let a little old blizzard interfere with my plans!"

Along the icy streets, through the snow, Daisy pushed her way until she reached the car line that would take her downtown to the meeting place where a new troop was to be organized that night.

Three girls were there when she arrived. "More will come," Daisy said confidently, "it's slow traveling tonight." And they did.

To help organize a new troop was an opportunity Daisy always welcomed. Gathering the girls around her--usually sitting on the floor--she would tell them, always in their own language, the story of Girl Scouting.

As she talked and watched their shining, eager faces, she knew that no weather would ever be severe enough to discourage her coming, no social engagement ever important enough to take precedence over a meeting held for a new troop.

Sometimes a well-meaning friend would say, "But do you think you should spend time and energy this way? After all, you have so many important organizational plans on your mind--so many big things to attend to."

These were the people who did not realize that Daisy loved the girls--not an organization. She would answer them patiently, "Nothing is as important as the girls themselves. I want to keep in close touch with them. It's what we can do for the girls that counts-- the organization is merely a means through which we reach them."

Sometimes a particularly difficult problem would arise, causing great discussion, even dissension, in a committee meeting. Daisy would settle it, "Put it up to the girls. If the girls want it, then it is right."

Because she did prize so highly direct contacts with the girls, there was nothing, perhaps, she enjoyed more than going camping.

Daisy would pitch her tent with a neatness and

dispatch that always brought exclamations of admiration. "This tent's old," she would say--she had two old tents she hauled around with her through the years--"but it still keeps out the weather. And it has the prestige of having been the first tent pitched on more than one camp site!"

From then on she relished every moment of camping, as only a good camper can--gathering the wood and cooking over an open fire--the long walks through the woods where she saw many things that escaped less eager eyes--swimming in the cold pools, the hikes, the games, canoeing.

When the busy day was over, everyone gathered around the campfire for the time the girls loved best--story-telling by Daisy.

With her talent for mimicry, Daisy could make a fascinating monologue of the simplest story. She never missed the humor in any situation--even if the joke was on her--and every tale she told sparkled with wit. Her sense of the dramatic gave every detail importance.

One of the stories the girls always wanted to hear was how she got the camp site up on Lookout Mountain in Georgia. Daisy loved this camp, and it was named for her--Camp Juliette Low. It had been an idea dear to her--a camp where leaders would be trained, living among Girl Scouts on Lookout Mountain as they would live among their own troops later.

She enjoyed telling the story of how she got the site as much as the girls enjoyed hearing it.

"I was determined to have the camp on Lookout Mountain, though I wasn't quite sure what site would be best. So I explored," she would begin the story. "I got a pair of sure-footed mules and a stout farm wagon, and where they couldn't go, I went on foot.

"One day, as I was pushing through the under-brush, someone yelled at me. It was the man who owned the property. 'Been a-watchin' you prowl all over my land--now what do you want?' he asked suspiciously.

"I told him. I told him about the Girl Scouts, the work we were doing, and why we needed the camp site. Before I crawled back through the underbrush to my wagon, I had his promise to give us the land.

"The only trouble was, he didn't want to give me the land I decided we wanted. I couldn't blame him much--for this is the most beautiful site on the whole mountain! But I argued him out of it, and all that remained to be done was for him to transfer the property to me.

"That sounded simple enough. But it turned out to be quite a day! The deed was to be at the notary's office, in the little town at the foot of the mountain, where I was to sign it. When I arrived, we discovered that he had sent the deed down without the seal. Until

the seal was affixed, the deed could not be registered.

"I telephoned up the mountain and finally got him on the 'phone.

"'No, ma'am,' he said, 'I can't come down. I'm workin' on the road.'

"'Have you got the seal?' I asked.

"'Oh, yes, ma'am, I've got the seal sure 'nough. It just slipped my mind to put it on.'

"'Well, I'll bring the deed up,' I told him. 'You wait there for me.'

"I had a wheezy old car outside, and as most of you know, I never travel light! In it were three suit-cases, four boxes of stuff, my crate of fruit, an umbrella and, of course, my dog. I still had to find room for the notary. He didn't want one bit to come along, but I was determined to have that seal affixed and everything settled on the spot.

"So away we went--careening up the mountainside, the luggage bouncing, the dog barking, the notary yelling something about my driving. I yelled back that there was no sense in hollering, I was deaf as a post. Besides, I'd learned in Scotland when you're driving an old car in the mountains, the only thing to do is drive fast and hold on tight.

"Suddenly we were stopped short by a huge construction machine! Then somebody called down from the top of the cliff above us, 'I'm up here. I got the seal all right. Can you-all get up here?'"

"I looked sternly at the notary, and called back, 'Certainly we can.' It was quite a climb, and quite a struggle. But a short while later we stood on top of the cliff. Even the dog made it! There the seal was affixed, the deed notarized, and the camp site officially and legally tansferred to me."

With the story finished, there was a short silence until another request rang out.

Among the stories the girls liked to hear her tell was that of organizing her first troop, in Scotland. Daisy would tell them about the Scottish troop in loving detail. "Years later," she would end it happily, "I was in London to attend a Girl Guide rally. Imagine my joy when I saw, attending the Rally, some of my first little Scottish Guides, quite grown up, and leaders of their own troops in Scotland."

Out of Scotland, too, came the ghost stories the girls always asked for. The castle Daisy lived in--so she said--was haunted. She could tell these stories so realistically that everyone who listened believed firmly in ghosts while Daisy talked.

When the stories were finished, someone always asked, "Was the castle really haunted? Did anybody but you see the ghosts?"

"Certainly," Daisy answered. "Once when my sister Mabel came to visit me, we had a costume ball.

Mabel stepped into an upstairs sitting room and was surprised to see a young man whom she had not seen earlier. He was dressed as a Roman warrior. A few minutes later, Mabel said to me, 'I have not met the handsome young guest in the Roman warrior costume. Who is he?'"

"I explained to Mabel that he wasn't a guest at all, but a ghost. He had lived in the castle for hundreds of years. Many people had seen him.

"Occasionally someone suggested that we might find a way of getting rid of him. But I wouldn't consider such a thing. In the first place, he had lived there so long, I think it would have been most unfair to try and dispossess him. He was a charming fellow, and did no one harm. As a matter of fact, he was quite helpful at times."

"You know," she would tell the girls solemnly, "there are people in the world who are actually afraid of ghosts. Usually these are people one finds dull and uninteresting. A ghost in the house greatly discourages such people coming for long visits."

When the ghost stories were over, the girls would beg for other favorites--and the stories went on and on until it was almost time for bed.

Then Daisy would say, "That's the last one for tonight . . . tomorrow I'll read your palms. I'll tell everybody's fortune!"

No wonder the girls were delighted when word spread through the camp, "Mrs. Low is coming!" But no girl there had more fun than Daisy.

$\mathscr{F}$ifteen
A RACE WITH TIME

Back in Savannah, Daisy rushed into the sitting room and cried, "Why didn't somebody tell me what time it was?"

"Why, it's 11:30, almost time for lunch," her sister-in-law said pleasantly.

"Oh, I don't mean time--I mean date. I have to leave Savannah on the afternoon train or I'll never get to London for the International Council meeting."

Lunch was forgotten while closets and bureaus were emptied, suitcases and trunks were packed.

"Telephone for reservations . . ."

"Tell them the dress must be delivered before three o'clock--I want to take it with me!"

"Have this pressed, Bella. . . . Pack that carefully. No, I can't see callers. I'll write them later. . . ."

"Half an hour till train time," Bill announced. "Is everything in? The car will be at the door any minute."

"My diamonds! Where are they?" Daisy cried. "They're gone. They've been stolen!"

"No, they're never stolen." Her young niece, like the rest of the family, had heard this anguished cry before. "Now think. Where did you hide them?"

Daisy thought, while precious minutes elapsed. "I know. In the walnut wardrobe."

Young Daisy dashed for the wardrobe. "It's locked."

"Of course it's locked," her aunt replied. "What good would it be to hide your valuables in a wardrobe and not lock it?"

"But where's the key?"

"The key! Where is the key? It's gone. It's lost."

"Get a screwdriver. Remove the lock. Twenty minutes till train time."

At last the jewel case was out of the wardrobe, slipped into a handbag. Daisy, all smiles, told each one a hurried but fond goodbye, and with the inevitable Pekingese tucked under her arm, dashed to the waiting car.

Nothing short of a major catastrophe could keep Daisy away from an International Council meeting, even though it often meant she had to make a special trip across the ocean to attend.

When, not long after the Council was formed, the first International Conference was proposed, Daisy's interest in the international side of Scouting and Guiding became even greater.

The first International Conference was to be held in 1920, in Oxford, England. The purpose was to bring together Girl Scouts and Guides from as many countries as possible.

The letters of invitation had scarcely gone off around the world when Daisy began to ask impatiently, "Hasn't anyone answered yet? Why don't they write and say they will come?" And when the replies started to come in, she received them with the greatest eagerness.

Occasionally a reply would read: ". . . Our organization here is so young. We regret to say we do not have sufficient funds to send delegates. . . ."

Daisy would cry, "Oh, but they must come. I'll pay their expenses myself. Write and tell them to plan to attend. Tell them I want them to stay at my home, as my guests."

To her delight, the first Conference was so successful, it was decided to hold a World Conference, or Encampment, every other year, the 1922 gathering to be in Cambridge, England.

Shortly after the second World Encampment, something else happened that made Daisy very happy. An American woman gave the English Girl Guides a beautiful estate, Foxlease, in the New Forest, for a camp.

This was important to Daisy because, while her

vision was to see strong bonds of friendship forged between girls of all lands, she was always particularly eager to keep friendship between the American Girl Scouts and the English Girl Guides firmly cemented. This was partly because she had brought the idea of Scouting from England to America, and partly because both countries were her home.

As she walked over the lovely acres of Foxlease, inspecting the cottages and other buildings, she said joyfully: "I have an idea. Let us set aside one cottage here for the entertaining of Girl Scouts and Guides from other nations. It can be a true symbol of international goodwill." She thought about it happily for a few minutes, then added, "I want to decorate it myself." So she set to work with paints and brushes, hammer and nails.

"Why, Mrs. Low--you can do everything! You're even a carpenter!" a girl, watching, said in amazement.

Daisy fitted the shelf into place. "Oh, I've been a carpenter for years!" she laughed. "When I was first married, my husband did not like the mantelpiece in one of the rooms of our new home. So I built another one. I decided then that I was a good carpenter." She viewed the shelf critically. "It needs a little more planing right here."

For two weeks she worked from dawn to dark.

When the cottage was ready, she invited the Guides in for inspection.

Pleased and smiling at their delight, Daisy said, "We're having a party, too. Strawberry ice cream! One of the favorite dishes of American girls, and a treat much neglected in England."

"What shall we name the cottage?"

"Let's call it 'The Link,'" the suggestion was made, "in token of the link of friendship between the Girl Guides of Britain and Mrs. Low's Scouts in America."

"I think that is a lovely idea," Daisy agreed, "and I know the girls in America will like it too."

Although Daisy loved Foxlease, she was disappointed when it was chosen as the place where the Third World Encampment would be held. She had hoped that maybe, just maybe, it could be held in her own United States.

The World Encampment was very important to her. She cherished deeply the ideals it stood for, and she found in it something very beautiful. For, at the Encampments, she saw blue eyes meet brown eyes in a new understanding. She saw girls from one nation exchanging little personal gifts with girls whose nation they had been taught to hate. She saw white hands reach out to clasp dark ones. And she heard words of admiration and respect where, previously, no communication had existed. This she wanted to bring to America.

Daisy had a secret reason for feeling urgent about bringing the Encampment to America that year: she was in very poor health. The doctors had been quite frank with her. "An operation might help. If not, it is difficult to say how long . . . ."

This secret she would share with no one. Not even those closest and dearest to her must know. She would go on, as long as she could, exactly as if nothing were wrong.

Since Foxlease had been decided on, Daisy was determined, in spite of her physical condition, to work harder than ever to make this Third Encampment a success. If she couldn't bring the Camp to America, she would bring something of America to the girls at the Camp.

So, as part of the program, she helped plan and present a pageant depicting the history of her country. A beautiful and moving spectacle, it told girls from monarchies and colonies, from republics and territories all over the world, the story of a great democracy.

When the Third Conference ended, everyone agreed it had been the most successful of all.

Almost a year later, on a gray spring day in 1925, Daisy was again aboard ship, headed for the United States. She walked back and forth along the deck, a plan shaping and reshaping in her mind. She had already discussed immigration restrictions with the captain of the ship. She had investigated sailing schedules. All that remained now was for her to convince the Executive Committee of the Girl Scouts that it could be done. This had been her dream for almost six years now--to hold the World Camp in America. Several times she had mentioned her dream to others. But the replies were always indefinite. "Sometime, probably. . . . It's a project to consider for the future. . . ."

Now Daisy's plan was definite. The next World Encampment, next year, must be held in the United States.

They would say to her, "It's too soon! Let's plan to hold the following one, in 1928, here."

Daisy knew that 1928 would be too late. The gnawing pain no one must know about was growing more and more insistent. The major operation--a secret she shared only with the surgeon and nurses--had postponed, but not cured. If she was to see her dream come true, the Encampment must be held in 1926.

When she told her friends at Girl Scout Headquarters of her plan, the questions were asked, as she knew they would be. And Daisy figured out answers that satisfied her.

"But where would we hold it?"

"At Camp Edith Macy, of course," she smiled. "It's near New York and convenient for all."

"Camp Edith Macy!" they chorused. "But it is four hundred acres of wooded hillsides. There are no buildings, not even water. The camp itself is still in the blueprint stage."

"Yes, I know," Daisy agreed. "There is a great deal to be done. Buildings to put up, wells to be dug, roads to be built, tents and equipment to buy. But everyone will help. All of us will work together. We can do it." She spoke as triumphantly as if the job had already been accomplished, then added, "In addition I want all the delegates to have a tour of America. They cannot go back to their native lands without seeing something of our country."

"A tour! But think what that means in planning . . ."

"Yes," Daisy answered. "That will be a little work, too--train schedules to be arranged and all that sort of thing. However, I'm sure the railroads will cooperate, just as the steamship lines will."

Still the women tried to persuade Daisy that it was impossible to build a camp and prepare for five hundred or more delegates from all over the world in less than a year. It would be wiser to wait.

"Don't put it off," she begged. "This is the time."

The pleading in her eyes, the urgency in her voice, reached every woman there. When it was put to a vote, the answer was "yes."

Daisy's joy at the decision was so great, her enthusiasm so contagious, that everyone forgot for a moment the appalling task ahead.

"I'll begin at once with all the correspondence," she said eagerly. "Tomorrow we will all go up to Camp Edith Macy and get things started . . . ."

Letters went off to all parts of the world, inviting delegates to come to America in 1926. Committees were organized, chairmen appointed.

At the camp, near Pleasantville, New York, workmen began clearing the land. Building plans were rushed, contractors hired, roads started. It was going to be a race!

"Will the Camp be ready when the guests arrive?" The question hammered in everybody's mind but Daisy's. Her faith in its completion by May never wavered.

When bad weather stopped construction--and it seemed the rains would never cease--nerves were on edge. When they drilled and drilled and couldn't strike water, tension ran high.

Daisy, sloshing through the mud, climbing over building materials, would assure them, "We'll strike water, you'll see. Everything will turn out all right."

Would the roads be finished, the Great Hall completed? Would the tents arrive in time? These were the questions the others worriedly asked.

At the last minute--when everyone had just about

given up hope--they did strike water. And by a succession of miracles, on the first of May, the last stretch of road was finished, the last foot of water pipe laid. Camp sites were built, tents arrived and the Great Hall was completed.

The night before the delegates were to arrive, a weary group of women gathered around the stone fireplace in the Hall. The huge stacks of new dishes were all washed. The cots were counted, blankets distributed. Food for more than five hundred people was in the kitchen. Perhaps, in some spots, the paint was not quite dry, and in the Great Hall there was a faint "new" smell of a just completed building. But everything was finished.

The task that seemed impossible had been accomplished.

Sixteen

FRIENDSHIP AROUND THE WORLD

The delegates drove to the camp in a long parade of cars. In the first car, proud and happy, Daisy rode with Lord and Lady Baden-Powell. Everything was right! The British liner Olympic, with delegates from many lands lining its rails, had arrived on time. Daisy's speech of welcome, made at the luncheon in New York where all the delegates met, had been warmly received. Now as they drove toward Pleasantville, even the weather was right. It was a sun-drenched May day. The dogwood was in bloom, startling white among the new green. The apple trees were huge bouquets. Gardens were bright with tulips, and voilets lay in purple patches along the roadway.

When they reached the drive leading to the Camp, flags added their color to the scene. The winding drive was lined with flags--a flag for each nation in the world, each one held high by an American Girl Scout aide.

That evening everyone gathered in the Great Hall, the delegates wearing the national costumes they had brought for the ceremony.

Daisy watched, smiling, her eyes shining. Leaders from India in softly draped saris, Netherlanders in wide, full skirts and wooden shoes, delegates from the Orient in silken kimonos, Czechs in gowns gay with embroidery.

They made a bright procession, their flags held proudly, as they marched around the hall. Each carried in her hand a bundle of sticks bound with fern. When she reached the fireplace at the end of the hall, she placed the bundle in the flames, saying as she did so, what her country offered as a gift to the rest of the world. . . .

"I, China, bring to the world her ancient civilization, her great philosophies, her exquisite porcelains . . . ."

"From the land of pyramid, palm and pylon, from the Guides of fourteen nations, I, Egypt, pray the prayers the Easterners do, 'May the peace of Allah abide with you . . . .'" "Scotland, my country, has for centuries past sent sons and daughters to settle in the lonely places of the earth . . . ." "From the rolling grassy plains of Uruguay, with its lowing and bleating flocks and rustling wheat, I bring greetings . . . ." So they spoke until every nation had made itself heard.

When the last bundle of sticks was placed on the

fire, the voice representing our own nation said, " . . . In the light of our world camp fire, we dedicate ourselves anew to the brotherhood of nations and the goodwill that shall encircle the world and abide forever and forever."

Then the voices of all present rose in song:

Day is done
Gone the sun
From the lakes
From the hills
From the sky
All is well;
Safely rest,
God is nigh.

The World Camp had come to America. Great joy filled Daisy's heart. She had never been happier.

When the World Camp ended, Daisy made plans to return to England. She knew there was not much time left. In England she had started to model a bust of her grandfather Gordon. That she must finish. There were International records to go over, people to see. She wanted to leave nothing undone.

Then she would return to Savannah. For there were things to be finished there too. Papers to sort, letters to write. Everything must be complete. Furthermore,

though she had learned to love many places on the face of the globe during her busy, happy life, Savannah was still closest to her heart. She was born there. There she had started the first troop of American Girl Scouts. Savannah was her home.

Juliette Low died in Savannah on January 17, 1927.

*   *   *   *

Seventeen years later--on another bright May day in 1944--a crowd of people stood on a pier in Savannah, their eyes on a ship, their thoughts of the woman for whom the ship was named.

The ship trembled. A bright spray of champagne burst into the sunlight. Swiftly, proudly, the S.S. *Juliette Low* slipped down the ways into the water.

"Ah, that was a beautiful launching," the Captain said. "As fine as I've ever seen."

"You may be sure Aunt Daisy wouldn't have had it any other way!" her niece and namesake said.

"She was a woman of great courage, with an indomitable will, was she not?"

"Yes--hers was a great spirit! And I am sure it will take your ship safely through the seas, in spite of bombs and guns and enemy navies."

Painted for war, slipping out of port always in the darkness of night with no lights showing, moving cautiously in convoy, alerted constantly for the sound of planes and submarine warnings, the *S.S. Juliette Low* took up the arduous task of moving desperately needed war material to our men overseas.

Liverpool . . . Cherbourg . . . Southampton . . . Belfast . . . Le Havre . . . Dover . . . Antwerp . . . Livorno . . . Rotterdam . . . Manila. . . . Into the shattered harbors, back and forth from the United States, the *S.S. Juliette Low* continued to carry her valuable cargoes.

When the convoy was attacked by U-boats approaching the English Channel, the *Juliette Low* came through without a scratch. The crew attributed their escape to "good luck." Then in the Antwerp estuary, a steady three-week attack by robot bombs sent many a good ship to the bottom, but not the *Juliette Low*. A short while later, off the English coast, she sailed safely on while the ships on either side of her were torpedoed and exploded in flames.

Now the men on board began to say, "There is something strange about our ship . . . something different. She has a charmed life. She has a personality of her own--a personality that was christened into her hull!"

Off the Newfoundland Banks, lost from her convoy, when her men saw two icebergs loom out of the darkness they wondered if even the *Juliette Low* could escape. She slipped swiftly between them, suffering only a few scratches where one iceberg brushed her side!

Once when her deck cargo of thirty-five-ton tanks tore loose in a storm, the Captain started to turn back for port. Then he thought of *Juliette Low*. Nothing ever daunted her. She would never have turned back! Soon engineers, firemen, cooks, messboys, radio operators, even the purser, were out with ropes, chains, cables, anything that could be found, trying to stop the tanks. When the crisis was over, and the ship was serenely moving on, the Captain said: "Your hard work secured the tanks. But it was her spirit that kept us going. Because of her spirit, General Eisenhower will receive his cargo on time!"

So, long after she was gone, the indomitable spirit of Daisy Low fought through another war and helped her nation win it.

When peace came, the crew of the *S.S. Juliette Low* heard disturbing rumors. "Liberty ships are to be scrapped. . . . They were built for wartime use only."

The men who knew the ship said, "That must not happen to *Juliette*. She is different from all the others. . . . Her usefulness will go on. She must be saved."

After months of suspense, official word was received. "The *S.S. Juliette Low* will be kept in service."

Now she began a peacetime service as great as her service during the war. Her duty was to carry relief supplies--food, clothing and fuel--to the homeless and hungry people of the world.

On one of her first peacetime trips, her hold filled with relief materials for a city which had suffered much, the *Juliette* ran into a heavy North Atlantic storm. Waves sixty feet high smashed across her decks. Winds as strong as 135 miles an hour tore at her, spun her around, ripped away her lifeboats, smashed her deck gear.

Over her wireless came a constant tap of SOS's, of urgent signals, from other ships. But none went out from the *Juliette Low*!

"Don't you worry," the men assured each other. "Our *Juliette* will make it. The same spirit that brought her through the war will carry her through in peace."

The ship reached port safely, her precious cargo intact for the people of Rotterdam. At port the men learned that many ships had gone down in the storm. Most of those that came through had lost members of their crew. But no man aboard the *Juliette* had so much as suffered a small injury!

From port to port the S.S. *Juliette Low* now made her way, carrying cargoes that saved lives and renewed hopes. Often in a foreign port, Girl Scouts or Girl Guides come aboard to greet her. Then the Captain conveys to them messages of friendship from the Girl Scouts of America, and serves them tea, "As Mrs.

Low would want me to do."

He tells them, too, of the courage and spirit of the ship, and how it lives up to the spirit of the woman for whom it was named. Through that spirit instruments of peace and goodwill are carried from America to many nations.

A spirit so great in strength and courage will never die. Today in the memories and minds of men and women throughout the world--but especially in the hearts of millions of girls--Daisy Low continues to live on and on, and to be cherished.

GLOSSARY

adders tongue	a type of fern or plant, such as the dogwood violet
Addams, Jane	a famous American social worker
amalgamated	brought together into a unified whole; joined
amicably	in a friendly way
Angora goats	a kind of goat with long silky hair that is used in making material
Armistice	an armistice means the end of a war; Armistice Day is celebrated on November 11 to remember the end of World War I which ended on that day in 1918
autocrat	a ruler with absolute power; or an arrogant and domineering person
bazaar	a marketplace or a street lined with shops and stalls where merchants sell their products
Benares	a former name for the town Varanasi

in India, sacred to the Hindu religion

brocade   a heavy material with a raised
                     design

capital   the money or possessions a person
                     owns;   assets

compensation   payment for work done

consternation   sudden confusion or frustration

cotillion   a formal ball or party where young
                     women are presented to society

Crystal Palace   a large building, mainly of glass, built
                     in London, England in 1851 to house
                     the first international exhibit

curriculum   the particular courses that are taught in
                     a school

curtsey   a gesture of respect made by bend-
                     ing the knees with one foot forward

damask   a richly-patterned fabric of cotton,
                     linen, silk, or wool

debut   the first public appearance of some-
                     thing, especially a formal presenta-
                     tion of a young woman to society

delirious   not knowing what you are doing;
                     mental confusion

demerit	a bad mark against a person's record
desolation	feeling totally alone or miserable
dissension	disagreement or a difference of opinion
dubious	having doubts; undecided or unsure
duck	a heavy cotton cloth
eke out	to squeeze out; to have a hard time making a living
elegantly	with refined or graceful movements or appearance
estuary	a part of a river where the current meets the ocean's tides; a channel
exasperation	anger or irritability
executioner	a person who puts another person to death
exodus	to go out
exquisite	really pretty
fascinating	very interesting
festoons	strings or garlands of ribbon or other material suspended in loops

flycatcher orchid	a type of exotic plant
foliage	leaves
for a song	a slang expression that means something comes very easily or cheaply
frivolous	not worthy of serious attention; not very important
gallant	gentlemanly; attentive to women
Ganges	a river in India, sacred to the Hindu religion
Gibbons, Cardinal James	a Roman Catholic churchman (1834-1921) who was the archbishop of Baltimore
grouse	a plump bird
haversack	a one-strapped bag carried over the shoulder for hiking or marching
hepatica	a plant that grows in the woods with lavender or white flowers; also called "liverwort"
homely	not very pretty
horticulture	the science of gardening or growing plants

incoherent	not understandable
indignant	to be very angry, specially over something mean or unjust
indomitable	someone who can't be overcome or conquered
infuriate	to make someone very mad
ingenuity	inventive or imaginative skill
iron-mongering	an iron-monger is a hardware salesman
khaki	a kind of material that is several different colors of browns, greens and yellows that soldiers' uniforms are often made of so that they can blend in with their surroundings
Kipling, Rudyard	an English poet and writer who lived from 1865 to 1936
knickers	long bloomers that girls and women used to wear as underclothes
La Crosse	a game of American Indian origin resembling hockey, played with a long stick called the lacrosse stick
launch	to start a new venture
Lenape	an American Indian tribe

leprosy	a disease in which the flesh often rots away
loin cloth	a small piece of cloth worn by men at their waists to cover the front of their bodies, like Tarzan
Lusitania	a British ship that was sunk by the Germans during World War I
macaw	a large tropical parrot
Madame Tussaud's Wax Museum	a museum in London, England where wax figures of famous people are on display
Mafeking	a former capital city of the country Bechuanaland now called Botswana
masquerade	a costume ball or party; to disguise or pretend
matinee	an afternoon performance of a play or show
meager	very little
medium	the specific kind of way in which art is produced, such as in painting or sculpture
messboys	busboys; people who clean up after a dinner

model	to make a small replica of something, usually out of clay (as in modeling clay)
miniature	a small painting with very fine details
nom de plume	a name that a writer makes up so that his or her real name won't be known
pap	baby food, usually soft and tasteless
paymaster	a person in charge of paying wages or salaries
Pekingese	a small pug-faced dog with long hair
perspective	in art, a way of showing depth by the way the lines are drawn
piazza	a porch or verandah, or a broad street or courtyard
Piccadilly	a well-known street in London, England
pittosporum	a type of evergreen tree or shrub native to New Zealand and Australia
plague	an epidemic of disease
pokeberry	a blackish-red berry that grows on a tall plant

precipice	a steep overhanging mass of rocks; a cliff
purser	the officer on a ship in charge of money matters
pylon	a huge gate or entrance way, or any large structure marking the entrance to a place
regatta	a boat race
renard	the French word for fox
requisite	something absolutely needed or essential
ride to hounds	to go fox hunting
sanctimonious	self-righteous; putting on an act of being religious
sateen	a cotton cloth with a satiny finish
scones	round, soft doughy pastry
Senecas	an American Indian tribe
Shawanoes	another name for the American Indian tribe known as the Shawnees
shoals	a shallow place in a body of water; a sandbar

silver nitrate	a poisonous substance often used in photography, the making of mirrors, or hair dyeing
spasmodic	jerky motions or coming in intervals
spring beauties	a North American plant with pinkish or white flowers
tantalize	to make someone want something really badly but to keep it away from him or her; to tease
tarpon	a large silvery game fish
tarts	small open pies with sweet fillings
tenement	a run-down apartment building
terrapin	a kind of turtle
tulle	a fine starched net of silk or other material used for veils
U-boats	German submarines
utter	complete or total
valise	a small piece of luggage
whist	a card game, the forerunner of the game of bridge